summer wisdom

Dedicated to St Erkenwald

summer wisdom

Reflections from the book of Proverbs

Eric Rew

Published by
The Bible Reading Fellowship
Peter's Way, Sandy Lane West
Oxford OX4 5HG
ISBN 1 84101 086 3

First published 2000
10 9 8 7 6 5 4 3 2 1 0

Acknowledgments
Unless otherwise stated, scripture quotations are taken
from The New Revised Standard Version of the Bible,
Anglicized Edition, copyright © 1989, 1995 by the
Division of Christian Education of the National Council
of the Churches of Christ in the USA, and are used by
permission. All rights reserved.

Scripture quotations taken from the Holy Bible, New
International Version, copyright © 1973, 1978, 1984 by
International Bible Society, are used by permission of
Hodder & Stoughton Limited. All rights reserved. 'NIV'
is a registered trademark of International Bible Society.
UK trademark number 1448790.

Scriptures quoted from the Good News Bible published
by The Bible Societies/HarperCollins Publishers Ltd, UK
© American Bible Society 1966, 1971, 1976, 1992, used
with permission.

A catalogue record for this book is available from the
British Library

Printed and bound in Great Britain by
Caledonian International Book Manufacturing Ltd,
Glasgow

Preface

A vicar once told me that whenever he went on holiday he always took with him six theological books and one novel. The theological books had been sitting on his shelf for several months and he was feeling a bit guilty about not finding the time to read them. The novel was a bit of light reading—he was going on holiday, after all. What happened? Well, by the time he came back he had finished the novel and not touched the theology, of course! I do not blame him really. After all, if the 'proper' books were that important he would have read them before he went on holiday— and I do not know what the family would have thought if he had spent so much time on holiday reading theology.

Why do I mention this? Because the hope behind this book is to provide some worthwhile 'summer' reading that is not too much like hard work and could still be taken on holiday. It gives a practical interpretation of an extremely interesting but often overlooked part of the Bible. Each section is short enough to be read in a fairly brief time and I hope that this means it will be particularly accessible to those who have not got down to studying Proverbs before. Although the sections are dated, it does not matter if you leave it a few days and pick it up again later. If you end up taking this book on holiday and have not read it by the time you get back, *it does not matter*! The idea is that you might start it sometime in summer, but it is not tied to particular dates, so you can start and stop as and when you need. I would encourage you to read all of it, though, if you can.

Although I have not covered every single verse of Proverbs, it is a wide and representative selection. By the time you have finished you will have a good idea of the contents and main themes of Proverbs even if you do not agree with what I say about them. I am not an expert on the book of Proverbs but I have a longstanding affection for it. As well as containing some useful ideas, I think it is fun too!

Eric Rew

Contents

Foreword

The book of Proverbs is unique in the Bible, for it has no storyline but is a collection of 'short, pithy sayings'—to give the dictionary definition of proverbs. These, however, are not folksy expressions, but words of advice and wisdom given by King Solomon and other contributors, on all sorts of human situations and the God-given manner of dealing with them. King Solomon was a very wise man, who had prayed for the gift of wisdom above all other gifts, and God had granted his request in full measure. Something to bear in mind for our own praying, perhaps!

Solomon also knew how to impart his words of wisdom and advice in what we would call today 'sound-bites'—memorable short sentences, easy to remember and repeat, and just as applicable to life today as in his day. The danger is, of course, that we trot out these proverbs without thinking about them, using them as shorthand to make our point instead of taking time to unpack them or bothering to look deeper into the treasury of truth contained in these sayings.

Summertime is a good time to explore this close-packed book of the Bible, to draw out and enjoy the depth of insight, human and divine. Eric Rew's book *Summer Wisdom* sheds fresh light on what maybe we take for granted. I have found as I have read this book that it has been like walking a familiar path with a friend, nodding in agreement, enjoying feeling comfortably at ease, and then suddenly it has been as though my friend has said, 'Shush, wait... be quiet... look!' And as I have peered in the direction he is pointing, I have made contact with something I had never noticed before, totally unexpected, and which would have failed to register had I not had my friend alongside.

At other times I have been brought up sharp by a perceptive comment which has made me almost gasp for breath, and has made me face up to something I had been trying to evade in my own personal situation, cutting through excuses and half-baked reasoning. Yet then, as I have accepted the wisdom of those comments and resolved to do something about them, I have been enabled to gather up my thoughts and intentions into prayer. The words I was seeking were right there for me to use and draw strength from. But I was also constantly nudged to come on further, deeper, to be more adventurous.

So let me encourage you to delve into the hidden treasures revealed here in this book. Take a few each day, give yourself time to mull over and enjoy them, and be prepared to be surprised and challenged too, as I have been.

Margaret Cundiff

Proverbs

This book is written in the hope that it will encourage you in exploring something of the wisdom of the Bible. It can be started at any time, though perhaps the summer is a particularly good time as, in the northern hemisphere, at least, it is a relatively quiet time in the church's year. It's when most people take a holiday, schools and colleges are shut for weeks at a time and even Parliament in Westminster takes a three-month recess. There is more daylight and a sense that there is more time in the day, windows are open more and generally there is less sense of being shut in. For many people, this time of year provides an opportunity to open our minds to new experiences and new ideas. After all, most people go away on holiday, even if it is to somewhere they have been before, because they feel the need for a change of scenery. For those people who have spent the rest of the year studying for exams or marking them, now is a chance to do something different.

Now is an excellent time, then, to take a fresh look at part of the Bible which we might otherwise be tempted to neglect. Proverbs is one such book of the Bible that is worth getting acquainted with.

King Solomon has a reputation for being wise. In 1 Kings 3, we can read that his gift came from God. He could have asked for power, riches or the death of his enemies, but instead he asked for wisdom. That must say something about the importance of wisdom in Solomon's eyes at least. There is also a famous incident when, faced with two rival mothers, he correctly determined to which of them a baby belonged. In the Bible, his success is attributed to his faithfulness to God, and his failures to the times when he turned away from God. Solomon is associated with the Wisdom literature of the Bible—Proverbs, Ecclesiastes and the Song of Songs in particular. When we look closely at them, however, we find that his name doesn't appear very often and it is obvious that other people were involved in writing or compiling them.

The book of Proverbs is actually a varied collection of sayings from different sources. Its final form took shape over many years and it has contributions from Solomon's court as well as from Hezekiah, Lemuel and Agur. Very little is known about Agur and King Lemuel except that they may have come from the same place. Hezekiah was king of the southern kingdom of Judah some two centuries after King Solomon. There are theories about how much was actually compiled by or for these people. For simplicity's sake, where a particular person is mentioned I would take him to be the author.

Not all of Proverbs is proverbs! As well as advice for holy living, there are practical, common-sense, shrewd observations, curiosity and humour. One important point to bear in mind when reading Proverbs is that it appears to have been compiled as a handbook for a young man who aspires to do well in a royal court—perhaps even an heir to a throne. Naturally this has influenced the choice of examples and illustrations made by the compilers. For example, Proverbs 25:6–7 is specifically about how to behave in the presence of a king. Their approach is not as inclusive as in today's society, where we might expect something about equality and fairness between ethnic groups and between men and women.

The book can be divided into eight unequal sections reflecting the diversity of sources.

CHAPTERS 1—9:	Proverbs of Solomon son of David, king of Israel
CHAPTERS 10—22:16:	Proverbs of Solomon
CHAPTERS 22:17—24:22:	Words of the wise
CHAPTER 24:23–34:	More sayings
CHAPTERS 25—29:	Proverbs collected by officials of King Hezekiah
CHAPTER 30:	Words of Agur
CHAPTER 31:1–9:	Words of King Lemuel
CHAPTER 31:10–31:	A capable wife

When studying Proverbs, we soon realize that there is a rich variety of sayings on many topics. Because of this richness, we can often find different proverbs saying much the same thing in a slightly different way, or something on a closely related topic, or even a flat contradiction (a bit like the English proverbs 'Many hands make light work' and 'Too many cooks spoil the broth' and others). The overall theme is the wisdom of God and how beneficial it is to anyone who wants to learn from it. Unfortunately for us, the proverbs are not arranged by topic but roughly according to source— Solomon's, Hezekiah's and so on. This means that you have to choose: study Proverbs in the given order or topic by topic. Commentators have to make the same choice. Here I have made a compromise by selecting a variety of the themes and, by and large, considering them in the order in which they are found in the biblical book. Each of the eight sections is represented. Inevitably the selection is personal and I am sure I have omitted some favourites—I have had to leave out one or two of my own. (Proverbs 25:20 is one and 27:14 especially: 'You might as well curse your friends as wake them up early in the morning with a loud greeting' [GNB]. As you might have guessed, I am not a morning person!) Some topics or related ideas occur so many times that it seemed appropriate to reflect that in the overall scheme.

The book is arranged day by day over a six-week period, with a short reading, some thoughts to consider and a prayer. The structure varies a little and the readings range from just one verse to half a dozen or so. I hope this gives it a less regimented feel. Unless otherwise stated, the New Revised Standard Version (NRSV) is referred to throughout.

With a little effort, the book of Proverbs is a worthwhile study, with principles that can be applied to our contemporary world. Why not join me in (re-)discovering what Proverbs tells us about the wisdom of God and what he may wish to teach us?

Week One

The fear of the Lord

PROVERBS 1:5–8

Let the wise also hear and gain in learning, and the discerning acquire skill, to understand a proverb and a figure, the words of the wise and their riddles. The fear of the Lord is the beginning of knowledge; fools despise wisdom and instruction. Hear, my child, your father's instruction, and do not reject your mother's teaching.

How can being frightened make you know anything? When I'm afraid I am generally busy thinking how to avoid or get through whatever is making me scared—I have neither the time nor the inclination to learn anything. So how can fearing God be any use?

I think fear has at least four meanings.

You can fear for someone. It's an expression of love and concern —you want that person to be safe from physical and moral harm. An obvious example is where parents are concerned for their children. Until a child has learnt how to cross the busy road safely, a parent will insist on holding his or her hand. As children grow older, the issues focus on things like where and when they can go out by themselves. However, the parents' concern can become unnecessarily restrictive and hinder the proper part of growing up which does involve some risk. At an extreme, the worry can get out of hand and become all-consuming, but behind it is always concern for someone you love. Yet God is more like a parent to us than a child, so we cannot be afraid for him.

You can be afraid for yourself. This fear is self-centred. It can be quite sensible, though, if there is a real threat. If someone is brandishing a knife right in front of you, the extra adrenalin flowing round the body might give you a chance of outrunning them. On the other hand, if you are always fearful, always worried about what might happen to you in the end, then all you do is to think about your own safety and you can become quite selfish. Even if originally there was a genuine reason to be afraid, I don't think God is expecting us to be selfish.

You can be afraid of evil or death. This is entirely natural and logical. Although Christians affirm that because of Jesus Christ we no longer need to be afraid of evil and death, the fact remains that they still both exist and are generally to be avoided. There are times when we do not have the confidence we need in order to stand up to evil but at the very least our fear tells us that there is something wrong, that something should be done to tackle the evil. If nothing else, our fear can be a warning about evil. But God is not evil, so it cannot be that kind of fear.

The fourth kind of fear is the one we have of, say, electricity. 'But I'm not afraid of electricity, I use it every day!' comes an objection. That is not quite true. Electricity is not inherently evil. It is very useful in running kitchen appliances, hospital equipment, transport, lighting and so on, but it is dangerous too. Pylons have warnings on them. We use fuses in our plugs and cover the wires with insulation. We earth everything we can and we stay away from electricity sub-stations and live wires.

We do not need to be afraid of electricity if we respect its power and treat it accordingly. I can change a light bulb or a fuse in a plug but for anything else I call in someone who knows about matters electrical, and I would never attempt anything like that without proper instruction on what to do.

The fear of the Lord is not like the fear of evil. It is the respect and fear of someone who has life-and-death power—beyond anything we can imagine. In the same way, we 'fear' electricity which can be both a domestic power supply and a life-threatening bolt of lightning. Without that respect, without that willingness to learn, we put ourselves in danger. At best our efforts will be futile (like a plug without a fuse) or at worst fatal (like trying to mend an appliance with wet hands while the power is still switched on).

The call to have a healthy fear of God is both to those who consider themselves like children in faith and to those who would regard themselves as being already wise to some degree.

Prayer

Holy God, holy and strong, holy and immortal, give us a healthy fear of your power and majesty. In your mercy and love, teach us. Amen

Wisdom shouting!

PROVERBS 1:20–23

Wisdom cries out in the street; in the squares she raises her voice. At the busiest corner she cries out; at the entrance of the city gates she speaks: 'How long, O simple ones, will you love being simple? How long will scoffers delight in their scoffing and fools hate knowledge? Give heed to my reproof; I will pour out my thoughts to you; I will make my words known to you.

Wisdom is a woman who shouts at us!

Is it possible to believe in wisdom at all today? With a few minutes in front of the television it is easy to come up with the answer 'No'. As we watch the news, we see war or yet another scandal, or the simple fact that people these days often look for their guiding principles in places other than in the mainstream religions. Some might go as far as to say that there is no longer any definitive truth or wisdom, only what each individual person believes. TV and radio debates seem more intent on airing as many different views as possible on any subject, rather than finding a consensus or sharing a concern to find the truth together.

The Bible presents a different view but not a simple, naïve one. It affirms truth and wisdom. It is positive in its view that wisdom is both desirable and achievable. The very beginning of the Bible shows God bringing order out of chaos. We can say, then, that at some fundamental level the universe makes sense.

Other parts of the Bible, however, do provide the other side of the coin by recognizing that life is not always as straightforward or as simple as we might like it to be. For example, Job presents us with the problem of unexpected and undeserved suffering, while Ecclesiastes' rather gloomy worldview is perhaps a corrective to being an overconfident believer. Meanwhile, Proverbs takes it for granted that there is such a thing as wisdom and that it is a worthwhile thing to pursue. Not only that, but wisdom is actually crying out for our attention.

One of the challenges of contemporary Christianity has been to include both men and women fairly in the life of the Church and to work out in practice the meaning of Genesis 1:27: 'God created humankind in his image... male and female he created them'. In doing so, we try to understand God even better. How do we recognize the inclusiveness of male and female in God's image without producing a picture of a bisexual hermaphrodite divinity? To begin with, we should remember Jesus' words that 'God is Spirit' (John 4:24) and realize that thinking of God the Father as a human being (even a big, kind, powerful one) is at best foolish and at worst blasphemous. If God really is spirit, then anything we say about him can really only point to that truth. Words are limited and whatever we say or write about God will never be exactly the same as God.

What we can do is to discover some of the characteristics of God and be prepared to recognize those which we tend to associate with the feminine as well as those which are traditionally considered masculine. God has intuition and feeling as well as logic. The Bible commends both knowledge and wisdom. You might think of one being more male and the other as female, I do not; the important thing is to recognize that God is the source of them all.

So why is wisdom female here? Partly an accident of language, maybe. It is certainly providential to find that the Bible does sometimes affirm the feminine in its imagery and is not exclusively masculine.

One reason is to do with the original setting of the book of Proverbs. In a number of places it is addressed to a son and its teaching is commended to him. We need to make allowances for that. It can still apply to everyone but we need to be alert to the fact that much of the book assumes that the reader is a young man. Behind these particular verses is the thought, 'Son, don't go chasing women. This Woman is better and she'll even go after you.' Chase wisdom. There is nothing to suggest that you cannot substitute the words 'daughter' and 'men' as appropriate.

Whatever imagery we use, wisdom is an essential characteristic of God who is the origin of all true wisdom. If we really believe that we have been made in the image of God, then all of us should be concerned about wisdom. And if we want wisdom we must go to its source—God himself.

To consider

1. Is it possible to believe in wisdom these days?
2. Why is it worth trying to be wise?
3. How do you go about 'seeking wisdom'?

If 'wisdom' is not something you have thought about before, then maybe now would be a good time to start discovering more of God's wisdom.

Prayer

Loving God, our Father and Mother, have mercy on us and in your mercy grant us wisdom and the perseverance to pursue it. Amen

Laziness

PROVERBS 6:6–11

Go to the ant, you lazybones; consider its ways and be wise. Without having any chief or officer or ruler, it prepares its food in summer, and gathers its sustenance in harvest. How long will you lie there, O lazybones? When will you rise from your sleep? A little sleep, a little slumber, a little folding of the hands to rest, and poverty will come upon you like a robber, and want, like an armed warrior.

Summer is time to relax and take it easy, isn't it? Put on your Ella Fitzgerald tape, put your feet up and listen to the sensuous lilt of 'Summertime'. Or perhaps now is the chance to get away from it all. If you can afford it, you go somewhere exotic to recharge those weary batteries or, if you prefer somewhere nearer to home, you choose a gentle walking holiday and the chance to enjoy the countryside. Or maybe it's the time to meet up with old friends. Whatever you decide to do, at least the holiday season is a relatively quiet time of year, isn't it?

There are plenty of people, however, who will tell you otherwise. Now is the time that fruit is ripening: someone has got to harvest it. For some people with seasonal work this is much the busiest time of year. And of course some work is every day, all year round: cows don't milk themselves, nappies don't get changed by magic and sermons have to be prepared too. Warm, calm weather, for some, may be a chance to sport the summer wardrobe but for others it heralds a season of hot, thirsty work, of becoming exhausted, running the risk of dehydration. While some tasks can wait for a more convenient moment—or, if we're honest, until we would rather do them—others remain urgent despite the temptation to take it easy.

The message of today's piece of wisdom is reflected in two

British sayings, 'A stitch in time saves nine' and 'Don't put off till tomorrow what you can do today.' I must admit, I find the tongue-in-cheek version more appealing: 'Don't put off till tomorrow what you can put off indefinitely'. Yet it is precisely that attitude that today's saying is warning us against!

Today's reading has an obvious practical meaning: to make a living, you have to work; to have food in winter, you need to harvest in summer more than you actually need at that time. There is no profit in laziness.

What has that to do with wisdom? Well, wisdom is not just about knowledge, being clever, understanding the truth or making the correct decisions. The proof of wisdom is shown in what you actually do. As human beings we generally reckon that we have a better understanding of the world than animals. So, if even ants have sense enough to prepare for winter without being told, so we should not have to be told to avoid laziness. Nevertheless, we are being reminded here that we need to work—and if we don't, we'll end up in poverty.

One of the tragedies of our society today is unemployment. For a few people this is simply a temporary state of being 'between jobs', and in the long run they are all right. For many, though, unemployment is a state of hopelessness, despair and poverty. There is little dignity in being forced to work but there is honour in being recognized as making some kind of constructive contribution to society. Not all work is paid work or fits the traditional nine-to-five norm and perhaps, as a society, we are not very good at recognizing this. As well as pointing us to the dangers of laziness, I think this proverb is warning us about complacency towards the unemployed too. There is no wisdom in laziness but neither is there wisdom in allowing fellow citizens' unpaid work to be ignored or for others to be left feeling unwanted, unneeded, with wasted talents, in poverty without hope.

To consider

1. Some people are under-employed and others are overworked. What do you think could be done to even things out?

2. What proportions of your week are spent on work, prayer, rest and recreation? How do you make sure you have the right balance?

Prayer

Almighty and ever-loving God, forgive our laziness and our complacency. Have mercy on our society and help us to include everyone's contribution to the community; for Jesus' sake. Amen

Creation and wisdom

PROVERBS 8:22–31

The Lord created me at the beginning of his work, the first of his acts of long ago. Ages ago I was set up, at the first, before the beginning of the earth. When there were no depths I was brought forth, when there were no springs abounding with water. Before the mountains had been shaped, before the hills, I was brought forth—when he had not yet made earth and fields, or the world's first bits of soil. When he established the heavens, I was there, when he drew a circle on the face of the deep, when he made firm the skies above, when he established the fountains of the deep, when he assigned to the sea its limit, so that the waters might not transgress his command, when he marked out the foundations of the earth, then I was beside him, like a master worker; and I was daily his delight, rejoicing before him always, rejoicing in his inhabited world and delighting in the human race.

I have great admiration for those scientists who set about understanding the nature of the world we live in. Even among those who do not believe in God (or who believe in one who does not intervene in the world) it is taken for granted that we can find out how things work and how they came to be. Geologists study how rocks are made, why there are earthquakes, how mountains and volcanoes are formed. Astronomers and cosmologists use their observations of outer space to help inform their ideas about how and when the universe was formed, about what makes stars shine, whether there might be life on other planets and what will happen at the end of the universe. In every sphere the scientists all make one basic assumption: that there is some kind of underlying order to everything. This order is not like a machine—the universe does not run like clockwork. It is more subtle than that.

In this reading we have an exploration of the subtlety of wisdom from a different perspective. It is a poem which celebrates wisdom as if it were an actual person. Some scholars have tried to make connections with ideas about wisdom in other Middle Eastern cultures, with Ancient Egypt or with Ancient Greece, where wisdom is depicted as a person or even as a goddess. Another view is that Wisdom is God in another form or perhaps something like the Holy Spirit.

While it may be informative to trace where biblical ideas and images come from, you can run the risk of missing the point. This poem is not trying to convince us that wisdom is a person, semi-divine or human for that matter. It is an assertion about wisdom's being part of God's creative activity and that God had wisdom even before he made anything. To put it crudely: God needed to have wisdom and did not (or could not) do or make anything without it. So what does that suggest to mere mortal human beings? If God cannot do without wisdom, can anyone else?

God did not put the universe together higgledy-piggledy. It involved wisdom at every step. The writer of the poem may not have had the benefits of modern scientific research but he or she clearly had a sense of wonder and an appreciation of how small human effort is in comparison to God's. What's more, this Wisdom character took more than a detached professional interest in what God was doing. She delighted in it. She found it exciting and wonderful. And that wonder extends to us human beings too.

As well as realizing that if God needs wisdom, then so do we, what else can we learn here? We may know someone who suffers from intellectual arrogance—the attitude that basically says, 'You can't possibly understand what we are discussing so you have no right to an opinion on these matters. They are too important to be left to the likes of you to decide.' Equally some people suffer from anti-intellectualism, that attitude which distrusts scientific and academic enquiry, especially if it invalidates their personal experiences and feelings. Either way, important discoveries (including controversial ones) and crucial decisions are either given the attention of a self-selecting clique or not faced at all. There are many issues facing us today, from medical breakthroughs to the production and use of energy, all of which affect whole societies and the whole planet. They cannot be left to a handful of people to consider and administer. Everyone must be involved.

Wisdom is for everyone, not just for God, not just for 'religious' people, nor just for intellectuals.

To consider

1. What important scientific and medical issues are in danger of being ignored by ordinary people?
2. According to the Bible, God took great care over creating the world. What practical steps could you take to help care for his world?
3. Think whether you would be prepared to give up a favourite activity, such as a holiday abroad, or a comfortable aspect of life, such as air conditioning, if the result helps the environment.

Prayer

Dear Lord God, you made your creation out of wisdom and love. You delight in your universe and in the people you have made. Grant us the humility to seek for wisdom, the responsibility to take our share of decisions and the will to do our part in putting into action whatever is required of us. Amen

Mischief-makers

PROVERBS 10:16
The wage of the righteous leads to life, the gain of the wicked to sin.

ROMANS 6:23
The wages of sin is death, but the free gift of God is eternal life in Christ Jesus.

There are obvious parallels between today's proverb and this verse from Paul's epistle to the Romans. (Do not read too much into the fact that the word 'wage' is used in one and 'wages' in the other.) Although the emphasis is different—one stressing the positive and the other the negative—the basic message is very similar: you get what you deserve. Sin leads to death and righteousness leads to life.

That philosophy is at the heart of most religion. If only we can work out what counts as righteous all the time, and avoid offending God by sinning, then we're safe. It is only right that good things should happen to righteous people and bad things happen to sinful people. But with just a few moments' thought on what life is really like, we can quickly see that that philosophy is not true, however much we would like it to be.

On closer examination we can see that the full meanings of the two sayings are very different. Both agree that sin goes with trouble: in Proverbs wickedness is seen to lead to more sin—you go from bad to worse, as we might say today. Paul goes as far as to say that sin leads to death. In fact, you earn it. Not only is death the consequence for sin but you actually worked for it!

Any action that leads away from God and God's truth, life, holiness, honesty and goodness is a sinful one. Thinking of ourselves as more important than God is the most fundamental sin of all. God is the source of all life, so if we ignore God, we are cutting ourselves off from the source of life. Eventually we are completely cut off from God—and life—in death. Some of the symptoms of sin are shown in our pride, self-preoccupation, self-indulgence, self-excusing and the like. A weakness for chocolate may not seem so very serious, nor any other petty misdemeanour for that matter, but they indicate what is important in our lives.

It does not matter what the activity is, nor how small it is. If it tends to keep us away from God or make ourselves the main priority instead of him, then it is a sin. The habit of self-centredness is natural and hard to break because it is one we are born with. It is easy to continue doing what we like and easy to ignore God.

On the other hand, our proverb sees the righteous person on the way to life. To be righteous is to live the right way, looking to the needs of others before our own, being truthful, moral, honest and good. For such a person their life is enriched, not necessarily materially, but in the quality of relationships with others and with God. Oh, this is so easy to type but so hard to put into practice! No matter how hard I try, there is always something I get wrong. I cannot always put it down to natural human weakness. Sometimes I just want my own way and have done with it. Chocolate or the TV are usually far more attractive than prayer or doing something else 'holy'! The natural habit of self-centredness always lurks nearby even if we do manage to diminish its effectiveness.

For Christians, the remedy is provided by God. We will never become righteous by our own efforts. We need God, but fortunately we do not have to deserve our relationship with God, nor do we have to earn eternal life. This is just as well, as no one is one hundred per cent righteous. On its own, this proverb may be true to our expectations, but it presents an impossible ideal. It is only in the light of the gospel that it offers us hope. Paul, writing in his epistle to the Romans, concludes that it is thanks to what God has done through Jesus Christ that we are not condemned to a fate of separation from God (Romans 8).

To consider

1. To what extent in your experience do people get their just deserts, with good things happening to good people and bad things to bad people?

2. Try to think of particular habits that, as far as you are concerned, are a sign of self-centredness. When can it be wrong to think of our own well-being?

Prayer

Almighty God, thank you for the undeserved gift of eternal life which you have given us through Jesus Christ your Son, our Lord. Amen

Generosity

PROVERBS 11:24–25
Some give freely, yet grow all the richer; others withhold what is due, and only suffer want. A generous person will be enriched, and one who gives water will get water.

Have you ever played the game Monopoly? The aim of this board game is to become the richest player by accumulating property and income while avoiding rent charges and fines. The winner is either the one who has the most money at the end or the only one left who has not become bankrupt. To succeed, you need to have a certain ruthlessness and deviousness—or a creative approach to interpreting the rules in the hope that no one will notice! It does not pay to be kind. The way to avoid debt or bankruptcy is to maximize your income by getting more property and accumulating more rents. There is, of course, a certain amount of luck involved too.

It is tempting to have the same attitude in life as in a game of Monopoly: only spend money as a way of getting more; try to avoid paying too much but charge as much as you can get away with; act as if the rules and regulations are just obstacles to negotiate—they have nothing to do with being fair or safe. This 'Monopoly' attitude can prevail in all sorts of situations and not just in business dealings. Do I want promotion because I will enjoy the challenge and feel able to take more responsibility—or is it mainly to get more pay in order to meet my growing expectations? Am I maintaining and decorating my home in order to keep it a safe and pleasant place to live in—or am I putting in extra hours simply to increase its value?

The Bible does not denigrate honest work, nor does it condemn people for becoming richer. There is only a problem when getting richer becomes our goal. Life is not a game of Monopoly where the pieces are just toys that are tidied away at the end. Although many people really do strive for more wealth, few people succeed and many become bankrupt and debt-ridden. In real life, changes in buildings or landlord affect individual lives in a way you could hardly experience in a game. And when things go wrong, you can't simply say, 'Let's play a different game.'

Today's reading reflects a different approach. It is possible to be generous, to 'give freely' and still become richer. On the other hand, being careful, even miserly, with your money is no guarantee against poverty. The proverb is not offering a foolproof formula, nor is it merely talking about some kind of intangible spiritual wealth. It is chiefly about an attitude of mind.

Consider two people, equally well off. One says, 'What can I give?' The other says, 'How can I protect my investment?' The first person has confidence and knows that they have enough to live on. The second is insecure, afraid of losing what they have got.

More profoundly, we are being asked to believe that generosity breeds more generosity. If we are generous in our giving, whether to strangers or to our family and friends, we will experience generosity in return. I do not think we are being asked to believe that some magic formula is at work here, nor some impersonal physical law of the universe. We are being reminded here that life does not follow the simple rules of a board game. Perhaps the rule, if there is one, is that the more open our attitude is in giving, the more open we shall be in receiving too.

'Monopoly' is only a game. Eventually it is over. Whether or not there is a clear winner, the pieces and the board have to be put back in the box. You hope the players enjoyed the game and are still friends at the end of it. That fellowship during the game should be more important to them than the game itself and the winning or losing. At least, that is how it should be, though people have been known to sulk if they have lost yet again!

Similarly in life, the way in which we have 'played' is more important than whether or not we have managed to 'win'. Have we been fair to our fellow 'players'? Winning at all costs can cost us good relationships and it begs the question of what kind of relationship we will be left with when the 'game of life' is over.

To have enough is to be rich. To be wise is to see how little you need to have enough. There is no monopoly on generosity.

To consider

1. When you are faced with a request for funds and you say to yourself, 'How much can I afford?' what do you really mean?
2. How important to you is becoming richer this year than last year? Why?
3. The Bible does not condemn anyone for how rich or how poor they are. How do you regard people who are richer than you or poorer than you?

Prayer

Heavenly Father, thank you for food, warmth and love. Thank you for all my possessions. Help me to be wise and rich; help me to be truly generous. Amen

Lies

PROVERBS 12:22
Lying lips are an abomination to the Lord, but those who act faithfully are his delight.

Much as I hate lies, I cannot help smiling at the alternative version to our proverb: 'A lie is an abomination to the Lord but a very present help in time of trouble'! It is very tempting to use a 'white lie' as a quick fix to get us out of trouble. Yet one of the earliest lessons that we teach children is that it is wrong to lie. I suspect that, for many of us, the lesson was brought painfully home when we were first caught out!

A lie is anything we say that we know to be untrue, when our intention is to deceive. Sometimes we may think that not telling the truth is the lesser of two evils. In wartime, lies are routinely told —propaganda, disinformation and so on, which are designed to boost morale and confuse the enemy. The intentions behind some lies are honourable where they are used to protect innocent bystanders from murder. During World War II, many persecuted Jews and others were hidden from the Nazis. If a friend said to a Nazi officer, 'I do not know where they are' in order to protect the innocent in hiding, that friend would be lying but also saving lives. The intention was to do good in general, and obey the commandment 'Love your neighbour' in particular. They did the right thing.

None the less, lying is still basically wrong because most lies are told not to protect others from mortal danger but to cover up our own mistakes and embarrassments or to get someone else into trouble. It is not always easy to decide on the right course of action. For example, if a colleague asks us to cover up for them because a mistake they have made might cost them their job, what should we do? They may have a family to support and we would not want to hurt them, would we? But once we start down that road of deceit, how do we know when to stop? It does not take long before we end up lying simply to cover up the previous lies. Perhaps a rule of thumb is that a lie might be tolerable if it prevents actual physical harm to our neighbour but it is not tolerable if it is to cover up some wrongdoing.

Sometimes we may fall into lying because we are scared or feel inadequate. This is most obvious in children, perhaps when they are starting at a new school and feeling lonely and uncertain in their surroundings. They may invent some fantastic adventure in order to impress their fellow pupils. They may say that they understand when really they have no idea what the teacher was talking about. Adults can fall into the same strategy too when they feel out of their depth. Normally, once we feel at home we do not reach for the lie so readily.

Today's proverb does not have our ordinary weakness in its sights but the habitual liar and the calculating liar. The first type nearly always tell lies, so that even on those rare occasions when they happen to be truthful we can never be sure and we can never entirely trust them. Calculating liars are those who plan their lies to get the best advantage, and they tell just enough truth to cover their actions. For both types, their first concern is their own personal status and well-being. Truth for them is important only as far as it is convenient. They happily turn a blind eye to lies if the lies do not disturb their own comfort and security.

A lie may be told to protect someone else's feelings, we say. But is that really the case? Is it not nearer the truth to say that we do not want to face the consequences of breaking unpleasant news? We are not concerned about the other person as much as how we are going to cope with their reaction. Giving bad news of illness or death can be difficult and stressful—there is no doubt about that —but we need to be sure we know whose feelings we are trying to protect. Maybe they are our own.

The problem with lying is that it makes it difficult to be straightforward and open in our dealings with other people. We may be able to justify a lie on one occasion or another but it always puts a strain on our relationship with God. And if we find that we are relying on lies more than we are on him, then we really do have a problem.

The alternative is to act faithfully, which is more than just telling the truth. It is also about *promoting* the truth, which means not allowing deceit to go by default even if we have not actually spoken a lie. In order to be faithful, we need to be in the habit of telling the truth.

To consider

1. In what ways can we be deceitful without actually speaking a lie?
2. How do we know when to tolerate a lie?
3. When we consider our own attitude to lying, how faithful to God are we being?

Prayer

Heavenly Father, forgive our self-centredness, our superior and un-caring attitudes. Soften our hearts and make us more loving. Help us to delight in truth and to avoid lying so that we may be a delight to you. Amen

Week Two

Speech

PROVERBS 13:2
From the fruit of their words good persons eat good things, but the desire of the treacherous is for wrongdoing.

At first sight the first part of this proverb may remind us of the non-biblical saying, 'The sweeter your words, the more pleasant it will be for you if you have to eat them later.' The meaning goes a bit further that that here. The focus here is not just on what we say but rather the outcome of what we have said. One way of looking at this might be to consider who are the more popular people: those who always have something pleasant to say or those who always say something critical?

Some people are encouragers. We can find this type of person at work, down the club, in the family or in the congregation. They are the sort of people who, whenever they see us, seem always to smile, to ask us how we are and enquire about our work or whatever it is we have been doing. If things are going well for us they are the first to say 'Well done!'; if things have not been going very well for us they usually still have something positive to say about us—often when we believe that we do not deserve it. They are always optimistic—even about us.

By contrast, we might expect the proverb to comment on critical people. But although they are less popular than the encouragers and can be disheartening to be with, they can have a useful contribution to make. Instead, the proverb singles out those who do more than simply find fault. They are the mischief-makers. They can appear at any of the same sort of places as the encourager, or indeed the critic, but their way of speech is quite different. If they ever congratulate us it is only if everyone else is doing the same, and provided there are other people around to see how magnanimous they are being! Ironically, they may not actually criticize us as much as other people do, because they are content to let others do their dirty work for them—but they will look on. When they do speak, whether praise or criticism, their main objective is to put us in our place and perhaps take us down a peg or two. Unfortunately it does not end there. The mischief-makers' own progress or success is far less important to them than watching someone else fall—whether by misfortune or by our own mistake makes no matter to them—and their building up or taking down of people is geared to that destructive end.

Rather than just trying to sort out the encouragers from the mischief-makers among the people we know, we should take a look at ourselves and see which one we are most like. Do we encourage others or do we delight in misfortune? We may not go around 'bad-mouthing' everyone—but aren't we just a tiny bit relieved when someone else makes the same mistakes as we do? Aren't we glad when we are not the only one to get into trouble / lose our temper / arrive late / get upset? And when the 'someone else' is that oh-so-perfect do-gooder who is so smug, don't we think to ourselves 'about time too'? Equally, we might not think of ourselves as particularly encouraging but maybe we make a point of saying 'Thank you' to someone who has made an extra effort on our behalf, such as a child at a school performance. Not all encouraging needs to be said—a person who smiles a lot can be a very effective encourager.

James' epistle in the New Testament notes how it is possible for the same person to say both good and helpful things, like blessings, and to be able to curse fellow human beings as well (James 3:9–10). It may come as a bit of a surprise to realize that the good person and the treacherous person may well be one and the same! If we are honest with ourselves we may recognize both the characters in us. That should lead us to ask ourselves some hard questions, both about what we say to other people and about what we really mean by our words.

Finally, we should not lose sight of the heart of today's proverb: what we say has consequences, some good, some bad. While we cannot have everything under our control, we can control what we say and we need to realize that what we say can make a difference.

To consider

1. Why might we say, 'Well done' to someone without meaning it?
2. How can we encourage someone without talking to them?
3. How can we tell the difference between the 'encourager' and 'mischief-maker' motives in ourselves?

Prayer

Heavenly Father, guard my thoughts and my words. Let me always be an encourager and never a mischief-maker. Amen

Worry

PROVERBS 12:25
Anxiety weighs down the human heart, but a good word cheers it up.

PROVERBS 17:22
A cheerful heart is a good medicine, but a downcast spirit dries up the bones.

The first saying might at first glance seem superficial and obvious. If you are worried, then of course you are going to be downhearted and sad; likewise, if someone says something encouraging it cheers you up. Sometimes, though, it is good to be reminded of the obvious.

Worry, concern and anxiety are not just an attitude of mind—they can affect your feelings too. We may have a proper concern for a loved one or about our own future. So we might spend time planning for ourselves what to do about our job or if a loved one is in hospital we might make plans to visit, for example. Of course, it is sensible to plan ahead, but sometimes planning for the future becomes a tiresome game of 'what if...?' What if the car breaks down, what if it is cancer, what if I am made redundant, what if there is an accident? This is where the real worry starts to set in: thinking about everything that might go wrong even though you have taken all reasonable precautions. To avoid having an accident in the car, we can drive safely, wear a seatbelt and never drink and drive. Of course an accident might still happen, but if we have taken reasonable precautions for ourselves (and checked the car) there is no point in worrying.

Health can be another big area of worry. After watching a spate of health series on television, I decided to take action; so I went to the doctor and asked for a check-up. He looked at me and said,

'The best way to be healthy is to be happy. Happy people do not get ill so often.' He also mentioned a balanced diet and exercise later on in the conversation, before adding, 'Avoid stress and that's half your troubles dealt with.'

It seems, then, that the saying 'a cheerful heart is good medicine' (17:22) is literally true, but we can give it a broader application. Perhaps the first thing to note is a distinction between cheerfulness and happiness. There is an element of decision with cheerfulness. You can decide whether or not to look on the bright side of life, whether or not to try to look for reasons to be hopeful. Happiness, however, relies on what happens. It depends on how pleasant our circumstances are. It is natural to be cheerful when good things are happening, so what about those ordinary, normal, run-of-the-mill times when nothing special is going on? Are we only going to be cheerful when something wonderful happens? Do we let our circumstances determine our outlook on life?

Having said that, when things really do go badly wrong for people and they are still being cheerful, then either they have remarkable strength and courage or they have not yet recognized the enormity of the situation! Shock or denial may delay their realization of what is going on. If we make the habit of choosing to be cheerful, however, it becomes easier to be hopeful when the going gets tough. Worry does not have to be our master.

While peace of mind and lack of stress are not a guarantee that we will never be ill, it is true that they make us less prone to illness and likely to recover more quickly. Stress can depress the number of antibodies in our system and make us less resistant to disease. It can also be true that our attitude towards other people and ourselves affects the way we treat our own body. A happy person is more likely to eat normally; a sad person may turn to excessive amounts of food for comfort or go off their food altogether.

Feelings of unease (or dis-ease) may be a symptom of jealousy. We cannot have true peace of mind if we are jealous. For example, what is the point of losing sleep over a nice house that we really want but cannot afford? There is no point getting wound up over something we want but cannot have. Such a state of mind can cost us sleep, patience and contentment. It can cause us stress which in the end could make us ill. If we are jealous, no matter what our circumstances, no matter how comfortable our lifestyle, we will never be truly happy—and in that sense not truly healthy either. A question we do well to ask ourselves from time to time is 'When do ordinary ambition and desire slip over into jealousy?'

What should we do? In short: be positive. If you are a worrier, do what you can to calm your anxieties but, above all, take them to God in prayer and leave them with him. There will always be some aspect of our lives that is out of our control or something we cannot predict, and worrying will not change that. And if you know a worrier, be patient with them. While they are wrong to hold on to their worries, they are often motivated by more than fear. Mixed in with it is a desire for everything to be right. This can be better than an uncaring attitude. Find ways of encouraging them and help them see the good that there is, rather than concentrating on the evil that there might be.

Whether or not we have peace of mind, we should always involve God in our affairs. We might wish to thank God for our peace of mind or ask for his help. We may need to pray for someone who we know is worried. We may even need to ask ourselves if we have a false sense of security. And as well as involving God, it is as well to talk things over with a trusted friend.

Prayer
Heavenly Father, I bring to you my worries and fears, my jealousies and envies. I let them go. I trust you. In your mercy, grant me stronger faith and greater love so that I may rejoice in your peace, and praise you more and more. Amen

Education

PROVERBS 15:14

The mind of one who has understanding seeks knowledge, but the mouths of fools feed on folly (NRSV).

Intelligent people want to learn, but stupid people are satisfied with ignorance (GNB).

When I first read this saying, I thought it was simply a statement of the obvious. Of course intelligent people want to learn, or how else could they know anything? But here intelligence and stupidity are seen not in terms of IQ but, as with much of the teaching of the Bible, in terms of the attitude behind the actions.

According to a biblical perspective, an intelligent person is one who realizes that they do not know everything and are willing to learn more. They may not in fact find learning easy, but they are open-minded, willing to check things out. As a result they can be more confident about what they already know because it has been tested by the new lesson that they have learnt. There are some Christians who seem to know so much more than the rest of us. We can point to the wealth of knowledge that they have given to us. Yet when you talk to them they claim to know very little and will eagerly tell you about their latest discoveries or the learning they are currently doing. Learning Christians are growing Christians.

By contrast, the 'stupid' person does not want to learn, although they may have a lot to say for themselves. You have probably met the type, that person who has no intention of ever changing their mind. When they talk, they can talk at length, without necessarily saying anything that is useful. You can find them in the queue at the bus stop, at parties, at meetings of all descriptions. They do not need a point to make, nor do they bother about whether or not their argument makes much sense. They just talk, telling everyone within earshot what they think—about the government or church services or education or what they have read or seen on TV, what is wrong with this or why that is good or why you should try this, and on and on. Sometimes they do let other people reply but they are not really listening, just getting their breath back before babbling on again.

Some 'stupid' people can actually be quite clever—they do have ability and can be found in positions of power. Pity any organization where the boss never listens and never changes an opinion even in the face of facts that flatly contradict him or her. For it is not just people who talk a lot who are the problem. There are also 'strong and silent' types who can be equally unwilling to learn.

There are some Christians who are unnerved by any change, especially when it challenges their understanding of faith. For example, as a child, I understood that the description of the Bible as 'The Word of God' meant that he dictated it word for word. If you hold this understanding, the discovery that there are variations in the manuscripts (inconsistencies if you like) makes it hard to believe that God could have had anything to do with it. What I learnt was that the Bible has come to us through many faithful human beings through a process of thousands of years. Yet in the end I realized that this only went to show how subtle and mysterious God's ways are. The Bible, for me, had to be interpreted in a fresh way but was and is still no less the 'Word of God'. Some people suspect that all questions bring doubt and that all doubt destroys faith. They hang on to their childhood understanding of God and Christ, refusing to explore what an adult understanding might involve. Such people are in danger of reacting in either of two extreme ways. One is to retreat behind a barrier called 'faith' which is really an arrogance that refuses to hear anything which in any way challenges their understanding of God. The other extreme is a reaction that involves not only abandoning a childish faith but abandoning the whole idea of God as well. They declare that none of it is true, that it is just childish nonsense to be dumped with the toys they have grown out of.

While the first mistake, being afraid to let go of childish ideas, leads to bigotry, the second mistake, letting go both of limited ideas and of God, leads to apostasy.

Many years ago, the curate taking my confirmation classes told the group that our faith and understanding would grow and develop over the years. He did us a great service. My faith has been challenged over the years many times and my understanding has changed accordingly, but God remains the same. Wise people want to learn because they want their faith to grow.

To consider

1. Are you ever prepared to change your mind on the basis of what you hear? If not, why not?

2. It might be worth asking ourselves from time to time: 'Why am I talking? Do I actually know what I am talking about?' If not, perhaps it is time to shut up!

3. If you are interested in being a learning, growing Christian, what are you going to do about it?

Prayer

Eternal God, thank you for the gifts of knowledge and the ability to communicate. Grant us humility and the willingness to grow in understanding in the knowledge of your love. Amen

Poverty and contentment

PROVERBS 15:16–17
Better is a little with the fear of the Lord than great treasure and trouble with it. Better is a dinner of vegetables where love is than a fatted ox and hatred with it.

When this pair of verses was written, meat was even more expensive than it is now. It is available to so many more people in our Western society than it was then in the Middle East. For the vast majority of people, meat was a special treat for religious festivals or other celebrations. In-season fruit and vegetables were generally much cheaper and more readily available. If you were rich you could afford to have meat more often. Who would pass up the chance to have meat which was so rare and expensive? Not many would refuse. A modern re-writing of verse 17 might compare chips with caviar!

The biblical writers do not have much to say about vegetarianism, except that they are not opposed to the idea and that in paradise it is the norm. (Look at Isaiah 11:1–9 and Genesis 2 if you want to check.) However, the message of these two verses is not about vegetarianism. Primarily they are a warning, posed as a question: is the offer of a piece of meat really worth having to eat a meal with someone who hates you? Is it really worth the hassle of sharing the same table with people who not only have nothing in common but also do not care for each other? The point is that good relationships are more important than luxuries.

Perhaps we should think of it this way. If a sworn enemy offers us an expensive gold watch, what are they trying to say to us? Perhaps they want to make friends with us and this is their way of making a start. In that case, the watch is just a token of the new friendship and not as important as the relationship itself. However, if they are still in effect our enemy, then their gift has a completely different significance. What are they really saying? 'See how generous I am being to you' is one possibility. 'You owe me a favour now' is another. In other words, we want to ask, 'Where's the catch?'

On the other hand, if a friend gives us even a modest watch, we do not normally fret about the question 'What are they after?' Surely our main reaction is one of pleasure. Even if it was not quite what we wanted, we are just as concerned about our friend's feelings as our own. Have you ever received a gift you did not actually want or need, but were glad to have been remembered anyway? Our relationships are more important than the objects we share.

My favourite meat dish is steak and chips, but my best meals are like the one I shared on a riverbank with the person I went on to marry. The entire menu was a bottle of Coca-Cola and a loaf of bread. It was the company that made the meal!

There is a joke that riches cannot make you happy so the rich person says, 'In that case I'll be miserable in comfort.' But the other side of the coin is this: if we have people around us who love us and whom we love, then we can be happy in discomfort.

One way of applying these verses is to enjoy the company we have. We need not spend too much money on food when the important thing is to spend time with those we love. More importantly, we should not disparage any gift given in love even if it happens to be cheap.

Prayer

Heavenly Father, whether we have little or much, let us be full of love and share whatever we have. Amen

Pride

PROVERBS 16:18
Pride goes before destruction, and a haughty spirit before a fall.

There is a picture behind this saying. Imagine someone walking along with his or her nose in the air. They are full of their own importance and are determined not to notice anyone whom they think is 'beneath' them. They are not watching where they are going, either. As a result, they do not notice the stone in front of them, so they trip and fall over.

The basic message is straightforward: if you spend so much time thinking about how good you are, you are in danger of missing what is going on around you. What you miss might be an opportunity as well as a problem, or a stumbling block.

It has been said that sin and pride have this in common: they both have 'I' in the middle. Self-centredness, self-importance and selfishness go hand in hand. Whether we think of ourselves as great or humble, the more our attention is on ourselves, the less our attention is on anything around us or on God. It makes it more difficult for us to see clearly what is actually going on. Whether we have our head in the clouds or whether we are busy navel-gazing, either way we are not looking where we are going and it is difficult to walk very far without either crashing into something or falling over. Our self-absorption cuts us off from other people. We do not have a problem with disregarding other people's need, for the simple reason that we do not see the need in the first place!

When I was learning to drive, I was worried at first that I might crash into something, and my gaze would always drift towards the bonnet of the car. I felt instinctively that if I knew where the front of the car was, I could be sure that it would be safe from any collisions. Unfortunately, as a result, I could not see far enough ahead, so it was difficult to take action soon enough to avoid such collisions. After a couple of near misses I finally heard what my instructor had been telling me all along. If I looked well ahead, not only could I see where I was going but I could also incidentally see things nearby. By lifting my eyes I broadened my vision, saw further ahead, and all without losing what I had been able to see before.

In a similar way, when we lift our attention from ourselves we gain far more than we lose. We cannot totally ignore ourselves but we do not have to be the main focus of our own attention all the time. Our self-absorption does not just give us narrower horizons; it cuts us off from other people and from God. It makes prayer more difficult because our prayers are either mostly about ourselves or because we end up, in effect, listening to our own voice, waiting for answers we have already decided upon. We need to lift our attention away from ourselves and focus on God. This is one reason why praise in our prayer times is so important. God does not need us to flatter him; it is for our own benefit because our focus must be drawn away from ourselves towards his infinite love.

Likewise, intercession—praying for other people—helps us to begin to see the world from God's perspective. Praying for particular people and situations is not mainly about getting the results we want but is first of all about sharing God's concern for the world and all that goes on in it. If we give ourselves pride of place in our lives, it is difficult to do that.

Today's saying is not telling us to hate ourselves. It is not saying that we have to regard ourselves as horrible worms or such like. It is about recognizing that we are not the most important people in the world and about realizing that other people are important too. Whatever our achievements, if our horizon is limited to ourselves we will not see very far at all. It might be an idea to spend some time soon praising God, thanking him for the blessings in your life and praying for particular people and situations where there is any kind of trouble.

Prayer

Lord God and Saviour, lift up our eyes from personal concerns, from self-absorption, from self-importance or self-denigration. Guide our attention to your wonder, glory and love shown to us in your Son and revealed by your Spirit. We ask in the name of that same Jesus and in the power of that same Spirit. Amen

Families

Proverbs 17:6
Grandchildren are the crown of the aged, and the glory of children is their parents.

Today's reading looks across the generations in two directions: from grandparents to grandchildren, and from children to their parents. Each generation looks up to the one before and looks forward to the one after next.

Behind this verse is the biblical writers' idea that to have children was a sign of God's blessing and, by the same token, for a couple to be childless was just the opposite, a curse. There was a very practical side to this belief. In an age where there was no social security system of benefits, pensions and so on, you relied very much on having children to look after you in your old age. Your security was in your children. They were also a matter of pride and honour, because the more children you had, the more secure would be your future. You might also become wealthier through having more people in your family available to work. This sort of thinking still applies in many countries today, though not, perhaps, in the West. To live long enough to see your grandchildren was a source of even greater pride because you glimpsed your own children's future and had some assurance that the family and the family name would last into the future as well. It was a kind of immortality.

Just as parents would one day come to depend on their children, so did the children depend on their own parents for their welfare, security and upbringing. With no compulsory State education or National Health Service, everything was down to the parents, even more than it is today. The whole family depended on each other at one time or another.

This kind of thinking is reflected in the fifth commandment (Exodus 20:12; Deuteronomy 5:16) where we are told to honour our parents. There is a promise attached, which says that things will go well for us if we keep that commandment. It may be simply that if we honour our parents then our children will have a good example to follow and will in turn honour us. The principle of the commandment is similar to the one behind today's proverb: that it is to everyone's benefit for every generation to have respect and concern for the ones before and after it.

Today's reading does not give us all the answers about how families should get on. In the New Testament, Jesus accepts children as people who are deserving of attention and warns against mistreating them.

The joys, pains and quirks of family life have provided fertile material for many a TV sitcom. The source of much of the humour is in the fact that no family is perfect and every member of it is a normal, flawed human being with his or her own interests and weaknesses. It is the mixture of differences and common life that makes families both exciting and frustrating. The Bible encourages family members to love and respect each other. There are times when it is obvious that we have forgotten that. When members of the family are hard work to put up with, it is very easy to think of them as an embarrassment or a burden. Today's reading is a gentle reminder for those times: each generation is the 'glory' of another.

For that reason, we should make every effort to stay in touch with our family even if they are in another part of the country. And whether we agree with other members of our family or not, we should always show them respect.

Family life can be difficult and sometimes relationships do break down irretrievably. Here, however, is the ideal that parents, children and grandparents should take pride in each other and recognize their mutual dependence.

Prayer

Dear God, Father and Mother to us all, forgive the hurts we cause other members of our family. Help us to cherish those who are nearest us, to protect the weakest especially, and to love one another; through Jesus Christ our Lord. Amen

Friends

PROVERBS 17:17

A friend loves at all times, and kinsfolk are born to share adversity.

A saying similar to the first part of this proverb is 'A friend in need is a friend indeed'. The assumption there is that the friend would not come to us if they thought we would not be able to help in some way. To refuse to help at all is to say that the friendship is not important to us.

Today's saying is about friends in general. Perhaps we should be asking ourselves, 'What does it mean to be loving "at all times"?' Surely it cannot mean having warm feelings for others every moment of the day? No, it does not. It implies being always ready to forgive, always making the effort to be patient, being gentle with our friends' weaknesses but not letting them get 'big-headed' either. It means having time for them when they are in trouble.

I wonder how Jesus chose his friends? As well as the apostles who went on to become leaders and martyrs in the early Church, there are some, such as Mary, Martha and Lazarus, of whom we know very little. From the Bible we know that Jesus stayed with them in Bethany (Luke 10:38) and we know that he loved Lazarus and cried when he died (John 11:32–36). I find it encouraging to see that these three have their own saints' day (29 July) simply for being 'companions of our Lord'. Yet, we could say that no one is good enough to be a friend of his. Perhaps the bottom line was not so much how good a person was or how much they might be able to help him but whether he could be a friend to them. Some did let him down, though several women stood by him at his crucifixion (Mark 15:40–41) and were the first witnesses of his resurrection (Mark 16:1ff.). These must be examples of what today's saying reminds us: 'a friend loves at all times'.

All Christians are part of God's family and are friends with Jesus. Some are called to be up-front leaders, preachers and evangelists like the apostles. Everyone, though, is called to be a companion of Jesus, to spend time with him, listening to his teaching or just enjoying his company.

Let's remember that friendship works two ways: someone else needs us to be a friend too—to be loving and caring even in difficult times, not a fair-weather friend. Our friendship with Jesus involves being faithful to him, and just as he is faithful and forgiving to his friends even when they let him down, so should we be to ours.

While we can choose our friends, there are those people with whom we have a close relationship not of our making, our 'kinsfolk'. That includes our family but might also include our closest neighbours and the people we work beside each day—in fact, almost anyone who is part of our life whether we like it or not. So there is another related question that we should ask ourselves in the light of today's saying: how do kinsfolk share adversity? Among other things, it means keeping in touch with your family through thick and thin. It means that in bad situations, accidents and catastrophes it is not just individuals who are affected: the whole family or group feels the impact of the situation even if they are not directly involved. So much the better if we can offer practical help, but sometimes all the help we can give is room to talk things through—yet even that can be enormously useful.

Perhaps our response to today's saying is to take seriously the need to make friends and to be a friend for others. We should be on the lookout for anyone who has few friends and be prepared to help our family and friends if the need arises.

Prayer

Heavenly Father, thank you for your Son Jesus Christ and that through him we have friendship with you. Grant us your love, so that we may be faithful to our friends and not abandon them when times are difficult. Amen

Week Three

Health

PROVERBS 18:14
The human spirit will endure sickness; but a broken spirit—who can bear?

Some of the healthiest people I have known have been wheelchair-bound and severely restricted in their physical movement. No, that is not meant to be a 'politically correct' statement to endear me to some fashionable social circle. It is a matter of fact. While physical health and disease are often beyond our control, what I saw in these particular friends was a healthy attitude. They were not defeated by their sickness although their bodies were most definitely restricted by it. They humbly accepted their limitations without either anger or self-pity. They worked round their limitations and got on with life.

Think of it this way: we are all born handicapped because none of us can fly. We do not have wings and, even if we could graft some on, we are so heavy that if we had a pair big enough they would get in the way. So what is the solution? Self-pity? Anger? Despair? No, the solution was a determination to get round the problem. It took centuries but now we think little of the fact that people can fly round the world in a couple of days or so. In fact, flying is not just commonplace but, if you live near an airport, it can be a noisy nuisance too!

In the same way, those friends of mine got on with life with the same determination we have whenever we go in an aeroplane. A lot of work is involved and it may be a hassle to get to the airport. The flight might be stressful—some of the passengers might not even like flying. Yet no one thinks it unusual to have to use a machine to get around. No one thinks that the passengers are anything other than a mix of ordinary people who happen to be able to afford the fare. So it is with those friends of mine—they happened to travel by chair!

A broken spirit can come about not just because of sickness but because of fear or despair. We may have lost our hope because of our circumstances—for example, being made redundant and with little prospect of employment later. Worse still, being locked up in prison indefinitely can break a person's spirit. Indeed, that may be the very point of some imprisonment—such as in the case of prisoners of conscience. Even when that is not the prime intention for imprisoning someone, we need only look at the experiences of the long-term hostages in Lebanon a few years ago, for instance, to glimpse something of how deeply dispiriting it can be.

Prisoners of conscience throughout the ages have had to face the situation in which their captors have placed them. One such person, commemorated by some Christians each summer (30 August), is John Bunyan. Most people who have heard of him will know of his allegorical story *The Pilgrim's Progress*. As well as being enjoyed by many for its encouragement to persevere in the Christian life of faith, it has introduced us to such characters as Mr Valiant-for-Truth and places such as the 'Slough of Despond'. What is particularly striking is that Bunyan wrote it during one of several periods in gaol. Like many people of his time, he suffered under the changing religious and political tides of the era but that did not prevent the publication of this classic, which is still among the best-loved writing of the seventeenth century.

So far we have considered people whose spirits did not break despite the circumstances. But what about those whose spirit has been broken? It is not easy to find the right words and actions to help. If I'm feeling particularly low, the last thing I need is someone saying, 'Pull yourself together, man!' Better that than to be ignored altogether, perhaps. For myself, though, the thing that helps most is if those nearest to me continue to love me and take me seriously. I know that they cannot feel what I feel and that their patience can easily wear thin but the fact that they haven't given up on me, even if I have given up on myself, can make all the difference.

In Isaiah 42:3, God promises not to let his servant break a

bruised reed or quench a smouldering wick. In other words, he will not permit that servant to extinguish what little hope anyone might have in themselves. For our reflection, we might consider in what ways we might help those whose hope is faint.

Prayer

Spirit of God, fill our hearts, our minds and our lives with your presence. Free us from despair and grant us true hope. Help us to be alert to those whose spirit is broken or breaking. May our confidence be in you, and may our attitudes make us a place where you can be at home; through Jesus Christ our Lord. Amen

A good wife

PROVERBS 19:14
House and wealth are inherited from parents, but a prudent wife is from the Lord.

Proverbs can hardly be accused of being 'politically correct'! There is not much in the book about being a good husband as opposed to the importance of having a good wife. One of the criticisms that our contemporaries have of the Bible is that not only is there a bias towards the life and faith of men but that where women are mentioned it is far more likely to be in a negative way than in a positive one. You only need recall Delilah and the downfall of Samson, Jezebel the wicked queen or the blame that has been attached to Eve, the first woman in the Bible, to get the idea that the Bible does not like women!

Although there are several positive images of women in the Bible and there are several female heroines of the faith including Sarah, Ruth, Esther and, of course, Mary, to name a few, it would be wrong to pretend that men and women get equal coverage in the Bible. Neither would it be right to ignore the kind of society that the Bible writers came from. It influenced how they wrote and provided them with the images and ideas with which they could describe God and his revelation. Although we may have different ideas and may even live in a very different kind of society, that does not mean that we can claim to be superior. Every generation has its blind spots and weaknesses, including our own.

When looking at today's saying, in order for it to speak more clearly to our situation we might want to read wife as 'husband or wife' or 'partner'.

Today's verse says that material things come from other people: the house and wealth that the heir inherits come from the parents and are a legacy of their work and good fortune. However, when it comes to fellow human beings, it is God who is the benefactor. Human beings are a gift from God, and a greater value is attached to the wife than to material things! This is a significant improvement on the notion that wives are just the property of their husbands—though the notion does not go as far as our ideas of equality today.

If we really take this idea seriously, it must affect our attitude to our 'nearest and dearest'. It is perhaps worth spending a moment or two to consider whether our treatment of other people really does show that we believe that they are a gift from God. And of course it is not just prudence that is a gift from God. Everyone is made in the image of God and marriage itself is a gift of God (Genesis 2). Do our priorities show that we really believe it? From the way some people behave, we'd be forgiven for thinking that their job, or football, or some other sport, or their car, or the television, was more important than their closest loved ones. We might ask ourselves: if we had to choose between those sorts of things, is there anything we would *not* give up in favour of our nearest and dearest?

Prayer

Loving Lord, the God of all men and women, we thank you for your gift of marriage and for all the special people in our lives. Amen

Plans

PROVERBS 19:21
The human mind may devise many plans, but it is the purpose of the Lord that will be established.

PROVERBS 16:3
Commit your work to the Lord, and your plans will be established.

I do not know about you, but I like plans. It is not just that I like to know what I am doing and when things are supposed to happen but it gives me a sense of being in control. I might not be able to control the weather but if I know the weather forecast I can plan to take an umbrella or time my shopping until the weather is more favourable. I prefer not to travel in the rush hour if I can help it at all, so I arrange my travelling accordingly. Plans can be very useful, especially if they save time trying to decide what to do as you go along. Elsewhere in Proverbs, the attitude is quite favourable to good planning and looking ahead; see, for example, Proverbs 21:5: 'The plans of the diligent lead surely to abundance, but everyone who is hasty comes only to want.'

Today's first verse I tend to associate with 1 January and the New Year resolutions that people traditionally make. They have all kinds of plans that often involve diets or giving up bad habits. Most people, however, admit that they have usually abandoned their resolutions before January is over and have gone back to the chocolate or the cigarettes or have left the gym club—although one or two do make it as far as March. In these instances it is not God's will that has prevailed but human weakness!

This first verse should be a salutary reminder to everyone who makes any kind of plans. It is not saying that it is wrong to plan, but you cannot plan for every contingency and there will always be the unexpected. It would be foolish to set all our hopes on our plans. If we are looking for God's wisdom we have to allow for the possibility that, however well-intentioned, our plans might not be what God has in mind.

Sometimes plans can be affected by more mundane matters. When I started commuting to work by public transport, I planned the quickest bus, rail and tube route I could find. It worked extremely well—until, that is, one section of the route was closed temporarily. I had to rethink all my plans and was irked at first. On reflection, though, I realized that getting upset did not help me or achieve anything—it just got me wound up. It was not as if the closure was aimed at me personally—it was for safety or security reasons. How could I then complain?

It is wise to plan, but it is arrogant to assume that we always know best. If we pray, 'God's will be done on earth' then we had better be prepared to give way and change our plans when necessary.

The second verse looks at the same thing from a different angle. If we read it quickly we might think it tells us to pray to God when we make our plans so that we get our own way. It most certainly does not say that! We are told to commit our work to God. In English the word 'commit' has the sense of 'trusting to someone else's care or judgment'. Here it means trusting God in whatever we are doing. It means handing over the worry to God; but without neglecting our responsibility. If we also hand over our work to God's judgment, it means that our plans will be changed into his plans. In practice it can be very difficult to discover what God actually wants. There have been plenty of occasions when I have prayed for guidance and the answer has been either, 'You have got sensible people around you; ask them' or, 'I gave you a brain; use it!' Often, too, I have stumbled around, keen to do what God wants, keen to do what is right and only later looking back, realizing that God was there all along, gently nudging me in the right direction.

The final thought that today's proverbs leave us with is this: it is only when our plans fall into line with God's that we can be absolutely certain they will be carried out. Because it is hard ever to be sure that we have got it right, we need to be open to the possibility of changing them.

To consider

1. How could planning sometimes get in the way of being open to God's Spirit?
2. How do you react when your plans go wrong?
3. Why might it be good to pray and ask God what he wants before you draw up your plans?

Prayer

Heavenly Father, keep us alert to your will and help us to serve you faithfully in our planning and in our actions; through Jesus Christ our Lord. Amen

Integrity

PROVERBS 19:22–23
What is desirable in a person is loyalty, and it is better to be poor than a liar. The fear of the Lord is life indeed; filled with it one rests secure and suffers no harm.

The interviewer turned to the head of the rail company and asked, 'Well, whom do you blame for the worsening levels of train service?' The man answered, 'I blame myself.' So the interviewer shot back a question asking whether the man was going to resign and he replied that he was not going to resign but he was going to do a lot of things to improve the service.

When I saw that snippet of an interview the other day, I was impressed. It is not often that we see someone in authority freely take the blame for anything. In fact, if they ever do, it is usually after they have had to resign. I do not think that the person in that interview was being cynical and pretending to be honest. By all appearances he was someone who took responsibility and did not waste time blaming others. In a few brief sentences he conveyed honesty and loyalty and gave the impression that he felt it was more important to do things properly than to make sure he kept his position. As I write, it remains to be seen how successful his resolve will turn out to be.

Today's reading gives us some insight into integrity as under-stood by the wisdom of the book of Proverbs. It includes honest talking and honest behaviour but is more than that. The dictionary definition also includes wholeness and implies something about holding disparate things together in a way that makes sense. Integrity does not hold incompatible values together, though, and its opposite, I suppose, is hypocrisy. By definition, people with integrity are honest in their actions: they do not deliberately set out to deceive. They are not the sort of people who say, 'Do what I say, not what I do'. They are the sort of people we can trust. They inspire loyalty, chiefly because they are loyal themselves. They do not use other people for their own ends but treat others with respect. They will not pretend to have one opinion while actually thinking something completely different. They will not agree with someone just to look good, but they might stand by someone with whom they disagree because they see that it is important to be loyal.

It does not mean that they will necessarily avoid being in charge or giving orders because if they are honest about their own abilities they will give a lead where they see it is needed. A person with integrity may well be the best person to have in charge because they will set about getting the task done without cynically promoting themselves at the expense of others. They are the sort of person who gets promotion because they have the skills to do the job and not because they have simply denigrated the abilities of others.

The 'fear of the Lord'—that respect and awe of the unimaginable power and authority of God—overrides all other fears for the person of integrity. They have their security in God, not in their status or popular opinion, so they are able to relax and get on with the job without worrying about the future or about gossip in the present.

While the values in the Bible sometimes seem to offer us an impossible ideal, such as the integrity described here, that ideal is worth pursuing. The more people who have integrity, the less fraught society becomes. Imagine the impact that a boss has at work if they do not have integrity. They are not totally honest. They are looking to promote themselves at the expense of others. They talk about fair competition but that includes switching loyalties if it suits their fortunes. Their fear is of losing their status or of not getting the next promotion. Anyone working for such a boss can expect little sympathy.

The boss who has integrity may not necessarily be all that chummy but they will be trustworthy and you will always know where you stand with them. There is a sense of security for everyone they work with because they will do nothing underhand. They are likely to take an interest in everyone's career development, not just their own, and will delight in other people's success. While they will stick to their guns when making tough decisions, they are more likely to be sympathetic if a fellow worker is going through a rough patch.

Integrity is not just for bosses. All of us affect the people around us even if we are not in charge of anyone at work. If our fellow human beings know where they stand with us, and know that we mean what we say, then they will trust and respect us even if they do not happen to like us.

To consider

1. Am I loyal?
2. Am I truthful in what I say and honest in what I do?
3. Am I trustworthy?
4. What do I need to do differently to have real integrity?

Prayer

Thank you, Lord, for all the people who live and work with integrity. Give them the strength to hold fast to honesty and loyalty; give them compassion in their relations with other people. By your holy loving Spirit, give leaders of countries, companies and corporations the integrity and gentleness of heart that result in leadership that is both right and kind; through Jesus Christ our example and friend, your Son, our Lord. Amen

Learning

PROVERBS 16:27

My child, when you stop learning you will soon neglect what you already know. (NRSV)

PROVERBS 4:13

Always remember what you have learnt. Your education is your life—guard it well. (GNB)

Why shouldn't you stop learning? Surely once you have finished a course, that is it. Once you have passed the test you do not need any more lessons. Why do you need to go on learning?

The learning referred to here is as much practical as theoretical, however. Often the best way to learn is to practise something, whether it is driving, cooking or learning a foreign language. For instance, I was shown twice how to use a particular routine on a computer but I just could not remember it. Not until I had actually done it myself (with my boss talking me through it the first few times) did I begin to really understand what it was all about and begin really to learn it. But it did not end there. I find that if I have a long gap before the next time I need that computer routine, it takes a little while before I feel confident about it again.

Today's readings are not just about being able to do day-to-day tasks or the skills you need at work. It is a reminder that it takes no effort to unlearn what you once knew. All you have to do is to stop learning, and what you already have starts to become stale and eventually forgotten. This is quite apart from the problem of whether or not our skills are up to date.

I am reminded of a story I once heard. A long time ago there was a man who was escaping from some terrible disaster in his home country. Eventually he arrived with some others at a port and found a captain with space on his ship for a few fare-paying passengers.

Now his companions had brought with them as much as they could carry and each had enough cash, jewels or other valuables to scrape together the exorbitant fare the captain was charging. The man had nothing but the clothes he was wearing.

'I've got more treasure than all those combined,' said the man and he promised the captain that he would pay double the fare if only he could pay him a few days after they had landed at their destination. The captain did not really believe him so he gave the man the least comfortable berth and shortly they set sail.

To cut a long story short, it turned out that the man was a scholar and teacher. After he had settled in his new location he was able to pay the captain back twice over as promised, out of the fees he charged as a tutor.

Originally, the story was told both to show how portable knowledge is (we carry it in our head) and how profitable it is too. Used as a story in a school assembly, the message is also 'See, it is worth working hard in lessons!'

Whatever the merits of that story, the Bible certainly does not recommend ignorance. We are told that learning (NRSV), or education (GNB), is valuable, something worth holding on to. It is a tragedy when pupils, students or scholars see their education as something to be endured rather than treasured. The more importantly we regard it, the more we will learn, no matter how easy or hard we normally find studying.

The concern of the writers of Proverbs is that we should lead lives that bless both others and ourselves. We have already read about how cherishing family values (17:6; 19:14) blesses both us and our family, how generosity (11:24–25) and integrity (19:22–23), for example, benefit us and others and how intelligent people are those who want to learn (15:14). Our learning can help us to understand the world we live in and to appreciate something of the lives of the people we meet. It can help us to understand something of the debates about, say, medical ethics that appear on TV from time to time. If, when we meet people, we talk with them in a spirit of learning, we are more likely to appreciate either the job they do or the place they come from. In this way we not only show respect but also allow trust to be built. Learning about our faith helps it to thrive and grow too (15:14).

To consider

1. How can we 'guard' our knowledge?
2. In what ways should we support those who are responsible for education?
3. How can we help in the education of others?

It might be a good idea to discover whether your local church runs any courses that may refresh, deepen or even challenge your faith. There are lots of books, cassettes and videos to buy or borrow, although learning with other people in a group can be more interesting.

Prayer

Lord God, thank you for all the people who have taught me during the years. Thank you for teachers, books, family, friends and a whole variety of experiences. Give grace to those who have responsibility for providing education. May they value truth, encourage integrity and display honesty in all they do. Grant me the humility to admit that I do not know it all and help me to continue growing in knowledge of you and of your world; through Jesus Christ our Lord. Amen

Justice

PROVERBS 21:3
To do righteousness and justice is more acceptable to the Lord than sacrifice.

This proverb reminds me of the writing of a prophet and a passage from the Psalms.

What does the Lord require of you but to do justice, and to love kindness and to walk humbly with your God? (Micah 6:8).

You have no delight in sacrifice; if I were to give a burnt offering, you would not be pleased. The sacrifice acceptable to God is a broken spirit; a broken and contrite heart, O God, you will not despise (Psalm 51:16–17).

Each of these passages gives us some insight into God's priorities. In a slightly different way they each say that what we give to God is less important than our attitude to him and how we treat other people. The sacrifices might be in the ancient sense of animals given to God at the temple or in the sense of the time and money we give to him, whether at church or to some other good cause. It is of no interest to God if we give him as much as ninety per cent of our income but never help our own family. It does not impress God if we attend every service at church on Sunday while using sharp business practices or being dishonest during the rest of the week.

Psalm 51 was written in the knowledge that God is more interested in us being honest in our relationship with him than in anything we could give him. Much of the Old Testament, especially the Torah (the first five books in our Bible), has as its major theme the sacrifices to God that are required by law. As we read on through the Old Testament, especially the prophets, we discover that God is actually more interested in a parent–child relationship, a loving relationship where the child is obedient not from fear of the consequences but from his or her trust in the parent.

While we are no longer required to offer animal sacrifices, this major theme of the prophets still speaks to us. They regularly criticized those who made much of their commitment to worshipping God but the rest of the time acted as if he did not exist—or at least as if he did not mind that they were mistreating the poor. Their real priority was their own material comfort and their energies were channelled mostly into creating as much wealth for themselves as possible. The prophets saw that when those rich and powerful people went to the temple to offer their sacrifices, they were being hypocritical. In effect they were saying, 'We love, admire and respect you' to God while they were in the temple. The rest of the time they were, in effect, saying, 'God who?'

The challenge for us is to consider what our real priorities are. Do we really behave as if God matters every day of the week? Are we really concerned to do what is right rather than what is convenient?

One area we might look at is our groceries. Yes, even the shopping we do at the supermarket is connected with justice and righteousness! Do we consider the impact that buying one product or another has on the environment? Do we think about how the food was produced and whether or not the workers who produced it were fairly treated? It is possible to buy some products that do less damage to the environment than others and to buy more fairly traded goods. So why don't we?

Another area to look at is the people we work with. We may not be in a position to give them a pay rise, but we can treat them with respect and kindness. We can make their well-being one of our top priorities, and this can cover anything from common courtesies to offering to help out when they have a particularly heavy workload.

Last, but not least, is the obvious connection with justice—in our courts. Whether we are part of the judicial system or not, we should all be concerned that justice is done. Of course no system is perfect, so we should also be concerned to see that miscarriages of justice are rectified as soon as possible.

The challenge of today's proverb is to do something. Why not seek out the more fairly traded products in the supermarket the next time you go shopping? Or consider supporting a human rights charity such as Amnesty International? Even today, consider whether the way you treat the people around you is a way that reveals your commitment to God.

Prayer

Heavenly Father, thank you for the sacrifices other people have made for our benefit. Help us to show we are grateful not just with words but also by acting with righteousness and justice in our lives. Amen

Wisdom

PROVERBS 21:22

One wise person went up against a city of warriors and brought down the stronghold in which they trusted.

There was a time when, every Sunday afternoon, you could more or less guarantee that there would be an old World War II movie on at least one of the TV channels. A frequent storyline involved a small band of heroes faced with great danger but an important mission. They were outnumbered and short of time—yet they succeeded against the odds. Hurrah!

I have a problem when it comes to celebrating military heroes because I do not like the loss of life, the killing and maiming that go with fighting battles. In theory I do not have much time for them, but I am a hypocrite too. I am not just grateful but I am pleased when my country's armed forces are successful. I only wish it were possible to win without loss of life and so much suffering. What is just as bad is that I relish stories of the 'We were outnumbered but we outsmarted them' variety. There is a kind of satisfaction if 'the enemy' suffer far more casualties than 'our side'.

On the face of it, today's verse is about effective military tactics along the 'small band of heroes' lines mentioned above. I do not want to belittle the very real courage and determination in the face of fear and mortal danger that those in the armed forces demonstrate. Fighting is sometimes the obvious lesser of two evils but it is still evil and I wonder if maybe we are not called to look beyond the obvious?

Be that as it may, today's verse can be looked at in two ways. Firstly, wise people will use the minimum of resources to achieve their ends. In military terms this includes having the fewest possible casualties yet still achieving the objective. This should be the aim of any commander, but for a scrupulous one the rule applies to how the enemy is treated as well—after all, Jesus taught his disciples to 'love your enemies'. This means that killing simply for revenge is not justified. Captives might possibly become allies; corpses cannot ever be so. The best strategy of all is never to go to war, if possible. If that is not possible, then it is best to get it over quickly, though that may be easier said than done.

Another way to look at this saying is to notice that it refers to one wise and presumably unarmed person who is facing a host of warriors. The wise person wins, but not through fighting or superior strength. We are left to speculate whether it was cunning, clever arguments, diplomacy or a negotiated settlement that did the trick. The key, though, is that it is possible for wisdom to overcome brute force. Whatever its shortcomings, the United Nations is a brilliant idea. Far better to argue with words than to fight with lethal weapons. Mind you, it is pointless to have everyone talking unless everyone is also listening.

The principle of wisdom rather than brute force, of using the least effort necessary to achieve the desired end, can be applied at a personal level too. Often a quiet word in private can do much to defuse a tense situation. If people are challenged in public, they are less likely to react positively and more likely to go on the defensive. It is possible to face a hostile situation and come out successfully on the other side without having to fight. The secret of such success lies in being confident but not belligerent, being strong but not controlled by fear or anger.

To consider

1. In the workplace or at a pub/club, what do you do when faced with an argument or a group of angry people?
2. What sorts of issues put you on the defensive? Why?

Prayer

God of power and wisdom, grant to all national leaders the insight to govern wisely and with compassion. Give discernment to those who negotiate for peace and justice, especially through the work of the United Nations. Be present with those in armed forces that they may put into effect Jesus' command to love their enemies. May your loving, just and peaceful will rule in our own hearts and be apparent in our lives; for Jesus' sake. Amen

Week Four

Reputation

PROVERBS 22:1

A good name is to be chosen rather than great riches, and favour is better than silver and gold.

On the face of it, I'm not sure I go along with this. Surely it is better to have plenty of money than to bother with being well-known? I'd rather have enough to live on than be famous. After all, what do we actually get out of having a wonderful reputation?

There are some in the public relations business who have been known to assert that there is no such thing as bad publicity. What they mean is that if a company or a product gets bad press coverage, what often happens is that people eventually forget what the fuss was all about, yet they are more likely to remember the company or the particular product in the future. For PR experts, what is worse than bad publicity is no publicity at all. On the other hand, if you can get a good reputation and win the confidence of people, then you are more likely to get what you want and more likely to be forgiven the odd mistake or two.

If we are honest, when we look at the 'communion of saints' we find a somewhat motley crew from all walks of life. There are some who were renowned bishops supervising wealthy dioceses (for example, William Laud), but also housewives (Martha), hermits (Anthony of Egypt) and even some who lived up a pole in the desert (Simon Stylites). Not many of them aspired to be Saints with a capital 'S' but all of them aspired to be faithful. In the end it is their faith that they have in common—plus lives that future generations can learn from. In that sense they have a good name as referred to in today's saying.

Take St Swithun, for example. Why him? Because his saint's day is in summer, on 15 July. Legend has it that whatever the weather is like on that day, so it will continue for forty days. If it is sunny that day we are in for a fine summer, and if it is raining it will be a wet one. A look at a set of weather records quickly shows that that is not always the case by any means. Interestingly, though, it was pointed out to me that very often the general trend of an English summer has been settled by the middle of July, so there does seem to be some truth in the observation.

What has all this to do with a former bishop of Winchester? During his lifetime he had been much admired and respected. When he died he was buried, according to his wishes, in a humble outdoor grave and not, as some had wanted, in a splendid shrine. However, when a new cathedral was being built a century later, it was decided to move his remains into a shrine in the new building. This was done on 15 July 971 and, so it is said, rain fell for forty days afterwards in protest! Thus the weather and St Swithun's day came to be linked in people's minds. What should St Swithun really be remembered for? The humility, simplicity and holiness that he represented were obviously the qualities that people most admired in him.

I do not think that today's proverb means it is fine to be in rags and go hungry just as long as we have a good reputation. Nor is it really saying much about the rights and wrongs of good or bad publicity. What it does prompt us to do is to question our priorities. Are we intent on getting rich or famous at any price? There is an echo of Jesus' question, 'What does it profit them if they gain the whole world, but lose or forfeit themselves?' (Luke 9:25). Given the chance, would we want to be the richest liar in the world, for example? It may be that our job offers us the opportunity to become a little richer provided we are willing to be less fussy about our moral scruples. Today's reading tells us that the good name that goes with integrity is preferable to financial gain.

Perhaps it is not fashionable these days to talk about having a good reputation or a good name. Perhaps the fashion is rather to have the illusion of a good reputation while maintaining money and other material wealth as a priority. Yet a good reputation may result in a better quality of living because it enhances our relationships with each other. Wealth may be able to buy good publicity but in itself cannot assure us of a genuinely good name. I admire the kindness and generosity in people of modest means far more than the largesse of rich people giving out of their spare cash.

A good reputation and the respect of others can only be earnt; they cannot be bought. They are valuable and, if deserved in the first place, more durable than cash or even a special shrine.

Prayer

Almighty God, thank you for all the blessings you give us. Help us to get our priorities right: to choose a good name rather than riches and to strive for humility, simplicity and holiness; through Jesus Christ our Lord. Amen

Equality

PROVERBS 22:2, 7

The rich and poor have this in common: the Lord is maker of them all... The rich rules over the poor, and the borrower is the slave of the lender.

One way of passing some leisure time is to visit one of the many industrial and rural museums that are around. As well as providing an interesting day out, they can be a good way of giving us some idea of history. Yet in order to be acceptable as tourist attractions (indeed, to be safe enough to visit), they have to be clean and tidy. In order for us to appreciate what we are visiting, there are displays and labels that explain the exhibits. Although we may find such museums interesting, we need to beware of gliding through and leaving with a picture of some golden age in the past or a romantic rural idyll. 'Life was simpler then,' we might say, and so it was— and shorter, too, with a huge gap in health and basic comfort between rich and poor. And the difference between ideal and reality, between the lifestyles of rich and poor, exists in many places today too; it is not just in the past.

Today's two sayings comment on the relationship between rich people and poor people. The insights are both theological and pragmatic. There is no attempt to romanticize poverty as a noble, simple way of life to be envied by more wealthy people. If we are rich, then we have an advantage over poorer people that goes beyond merely owning more possessions. But what do we mean by 'rich'?

If you are comfortably off, if you have anything more than enough to live on, then you are rich in global terms—the rest is a matter of degree. What are the symptoms of being rich? Having enough to eat, having enough money to pay the bills, being able to afford any kind of holiday, having some savings and so on.

Whether it is plain home cooking or eating out, whether you live in a flat or in a mansion, whether you have a hundred pounds in savings or a million pounds: all this is a matter of degree.

How can we lump, say, a multi-millionaire together with a council worker living in his or her ex-council house? We can do it when we see people's circumstances determined by not always having enough to eat; when 'saving' means keeping leftovers from one meal to use in the next one; when money has to be borrowed to pay debts; or when a 'water shortage' means walking ten miles for a bucket of muddy water—not a hose-pipe ban.

Whichever category we fall into, rich or poor, it is tempting to condemn the other. We might say that they are lazy or lucky or greedy or that they would never cope with our situation. Today's first saying challenges that way of thinking. We are told not to be a snob—or an inverted snob. God is the creator of everyone, whatever their weaknesses, their sins or their situation, be it rich or poor. God loves everyone and wants the best for them.

The second proverb observes a fact of life. Rich people, by the simple virtue of having more resources at their disposal, do indeed wield power over those who have less. The one with money to spend has 'purchasing power' over the one with something to sell, over the other person who is hoping to make some money. The people with the power to hire and fire can exert influence on their employees. We say that whoever 'pays the piper calls the tune'.

It also works that way in companies where a handful of shareholders own most of the shares between them while dozens of small shareholders own just a tiny fraction in comparison. The system is that of 'one share, one vote' so the more shares you have, the more influence you have. It is not democratic in the 'one person, one vote' sense and does not pretend to be. The original idea was that people risking most money should have most say in how the company was run. If the few with the most shares are wise and fair, it may not be such an unfair system. But if they are ignorant, biased, greedy, narrow-minded or just plain foolish, then the system makes it difficult for others, such as the small shareholders, to have much influence.

The same principle works between nations. Mostly it is the richest nations that have the loudest voices—not the biggest or the wisest ones but those that can influence international markets with their 'purchasing power'.

But there is an even stronger influence: debt. The bank or mortgage-lender has an effect on the daily lives of millions in this country, for example. The interest they charge has a direct effect on how much money families have to spend. If there is a problem with the economy, such as rising inflation, then up go interest rates and up go the payments to the bank. If a family falls behind in paying the loan, the lender has the ultimate sanction of repossessing their home. Paying off the mortgage or at least keeping up with the interest is the main financial goal in many a family. It is right to be responsible and to do your best to avoid getting into debts—or, if you cannot avoid debts, to pay them off as quickly as possible.

There is a similar power of debt relationship between many rich and poor countries. In some poor countries the total annual income is not enough to pay the interest and the result is a lack of funds for basics like water supply, hospitals and schools. As I write, I am aware that overall the total debt repayments to the rich countries are at least four times higher than the aid given to the poor countries. It is very much the case that with countries, as with individuals, the borrower is the slave of the lender.

To consider

1. How should the prayer 'Forgive us our debt as we forgive those who are in debt to us' be put into practice both between individuals and between countries?
2. When might it be wrong to lend money?
3. What kind of investments might it be wrong to take up?
4. How rich is too rich?

A practical response to today's saying would be to support one of the charities which are making a difference to the lives of poor people around the world: Oxfam, CAFOD, **TEAR**FUND, Save the

Children or Christian Aid, for example. Regular financial support can help charities plan ahead but there are also campaigning, letter writing, volunteer support and other tasks to help with. Why not contact a local representative of one of those charities and offer some help? You do not have to be rich to make a difference.

Prayer

Our Father in heaven, maker of rich and poor, weak and strong; your name is holy, your kingdom is coming. Forgive us our debts as we forgive those who are in debt to us. Give us eyes to recognize everyone as your children and grant us grace to act accordingly; in the name of your Son, Jesus Christ. Amen

Children

PROVERBS 22:6
Train children in the right way, and when old, they will not stray.

The biggest influence on children is their home—wherever that is and whoever looks after them. That place and the people there provide assumptions that are taken for granted, assumptions that may not be noticed until they come into conflict with someone else's. This is not to deny other influences such as friends, television and school, or to ignore the fact that as children grow up they begin to find their own way of doing things. Yet it is true that habits and values picked up when very young are hard to change and are deeply rooted.

I have an aversion to betting shops. Is this because I have a carefully argued theological objection to them? I could certainly provide one along the lines of 'The love of money is the root of all evil'. That is not the true origin of my feelings against them, however. They stem from some afternoons at the window with my grandmother looking across the road at the betting shop. Every time a man went in or out she would say something like, 'Naughty man, no money in his pocket' even if he was obviously putting his winnings away! I learnt that it was wrong to go into betting shops and that people who went in could well end up without any money.

The 'training' in today's verse is not specifically about education. It is more to do with morality than knowledge. It is both a word of warning and one of encouragement. The warning is that the wrong example to a child can lead to problems in later life. For example, it has been said that abusers of children were often themselves abused as children. They simply carry on with what they were brought up with. There are other less traumatic examples but the principle is the same: how we treat children affects how they will behave when they grow up.

The encouragement is that good values and wise teaching early in life do stick. This is so whether we mean the simple politeness of saying 'please' and 'thank you' or the fostering of virtues like kindness and respect for other people. It is not unusual for adolescents and youths to rebel against their parents, family or society. It is part of growing up that they must come to terms with their own identity and start taking responsibility for their own decisions. In learning to decide for themselves, they can easily make the wrong choices. In the end, though, the early values usually resurface.

Does this mean that we are doomed to make the mistakes created in our childhood? Not necessarily. We may not be able to change the past but with the help of God's Spirit we can change the effect that the past has on us. It may be difficult but not impossible. Thanks to God, who forgives all things, even if we were 'trained in the wrong way' we are not condemned to live by it.

By and large the Old Testament does not give much status to children. Until they came of age they very much depended on the disposition of their parents. Jesus raises the status of children and recognizes them as individuals (Matthew 18:1–10 and Mark 10:13–16). In today's proverb we have an affirmation of the value of children in their own right. They are worth taking time and trouble over. Their upbringing should not be left to chance and they certainly should not be neglected, left to fend for themselves. It really does matter how we treat children, but not because of some romantic notion of childhood. It matters because they matter to God, who loves them and is concerned about their well-being.

Today's reading is certainly not a charter for spoiling children. Nor is it about being especially strict either. The emphasis is on the right way. For Christians that includes virtues like honesty, kindness and love. And, of course, if we adults hope to train children in that way, then surely the same behaviour is to be expected of us.

To consider

1. What do you think 'training' should include?
2. Given the importance and difficulty of the task, how can we support those who train children?

Prayer

Lord God, forgive us the mistakes and bad habits of the past. Give us your grace to walk in your way and live in your love. Guide with wisdom and compassion everyone who is involved in the up-bringing of children and protect those in their care; in the name of Christ. Amen

Greed

PROVERBS 23:6–8

Do not eat the bread of the stingy; do not desire their delicacies; for like a hair in the throat, so are they. 'Eat and drink!' they say to you; but they do not mean it. You will vomit up the little you have eaten, and you will waste your pleasant words.

No summer garden party I have attended has ever seemed to me to fit the situation the writer has in mind. I am not quite sure why anyone would throw up after a meal if all that has happened is that the host has been a bit stingy. Perhaps it's an exaggerated way of showing disgust. Perhaps the temptation for us as guests is to eat so much as a kind of compensation for the fact that the host is rather sparing with the portions—and in the end we're sick from over-eating.

I was not sure whether to give the title to today's saying as 'Greed' or 'Stinginess'. Whichever is the more appropriate, the motive behind these verses is a comment on false generosity. Greed is not just wanting more than your fair share or grabbing all that you can get without any thought for other people. Some greed is obvious—the child who never shares their sweets but always makes a grab when any are on offer; the person who says 'The government should help' but who never gives to charity even though they could well afford to do so; the person who always finds reasons for receiving but never offers anything. These sorts of people are fairly easy to spot. They take but never give. But there is another kind of greedy person who does sometimes give and we might not realize at first that they are in fact greedy.

The picture here is of going to some kind of party, perhaps at someone's house. Now at nearly every party I attend, the host has two particular worries: will everyone enjoy themselves and is there enough food? It is very likely that they need not have worried because, whether they are rich or poor, they have provided more than enough food and there is likely to be some left over. To be on the safe side, most hosts provide just a little bit more than is necessary and would prefer that their guests have a bit too much, rather than that they should go away even a tiny bit hungry.

In this particular case, the host is more concerned about *appearing* generous. They want to look good at the lowest possible price. They provide expensive delicacies but not very many of them. They are worried that their guests might eat too much, hoping that they will be satisfied with as little as possible. This is not a desperately poor person sharing what little they have. This is a comfortable person out to impress. Once the guests realize that they are being used, it 'leaves a bad taste in the mouth', as the saying goes.

Have you ever had the misfortune of swallowing a hair? It is bad enough finding a strand of hair in your mouth and trying to locate and remove it. Although it is small, it irritates and gets in the way of eating and talking. It can be so uncomfortable that you forget about etiquette while you stick your fingers in your mouth in an attempt to get it out! But if you swallow a hair, and it gets stuck in your throat, the feeling is even worse because you cannot reach it. Perhaps that is what the dinner party of a stingy person feels like according to Proverbs. Alternatively, it might be equivalent to 'two fingers down the throat' because stingy people are so nauseating.

What should we say to this stingy person? 'If you cannot afford to be generous, then don't have a party, or don't invite so many guests, or don't pretend to be generous—do not call a snack "dinner"—or do share the effort, cost and honours with other people.'

Jesus made a particular criticism about throwing parties, which we should consider here. He asked what was the point of inviting people who were going to invite you back to their own party later. There was nothing special in that kind of party. The kind of party that Jesus wants his disciples to throw is one where there is no chance of the guests returning the favour. Jesus wants us to imitate

God's generosity by inviting people to our parties who are unlikely ever to be able to return the compliment. After all, God's grace is about giving us what we could never earn—an invitation to the heavenly banquet. We have no chance of returning that favour to God. There is an immediate benefit to this kind of approach. If we are not out to impress people with our generosity, nor concerned to get invited back, then we can relax and enjoy the party because we know we have nothing to prove.

Of course there are plenty of people whom we invite and who will after all invite us to their parties—our family and close friends. But then surely the whole point of the party is an excuse to get together, rather than about impressing anyone.

A practical response: next time you throw a party, check the guest list. How about inviting someone you do not know very well? Or someone who is not very popular and perhaps does not go to many parties at all? It may be a chance for you to learn a little more about God's grace.

Prayer

Heavenly Father, thank you for all the fun we can have at parties and the times when we share a meal with people we love. Help us to be generous in our turn and to include people who might otherwise be left out. We ask this in the name of your Son, who has invited us to your heavenly banquet. Amen

Envy

PROVERBS 23:15–18

My child, if your heart is wise, my heart too will be glad. My soul will rejoice when your lips speak what is right. Do not let your heart envy sinners, but always continue in the fear of the Lord. Surely there is a future, and your hope will not be cut off.

Each year we may get all kinds of postcards from people on holiday. They might bear the traditional greeting 'Wish you were here' and if it is a particularly nice-looking place I want to say, 'So do I!' One postcard that I was sent recently had a picture of three fields, one red, one yellow and one green, with a fence dividing the yellow and green sides. One cow is saying to the other 'OK, you were right, the grass is greener here.' It was poking gentle fun at those of us who envy other people. Envy can rear its ugly head at any time of year but in the summer it may be particularly acute with regard to the different holidays people go on.

I used to collect postcards of all the places I visited, on the grounds that if I got half a dozen or so it would save the trouble of taking lots of photographs. The disadvantage, of course, was that the places were never quite the same as the picture—in the postcards the sun always shone and the sky was blue, or the picture was taken from the air or some other angle that was impossible for visitors to see.

Of course, the main point of postcards is to provide a cheap and cheerful way of dropping a line or two to friends and relatives while on holiday. It's a good way of showing that we have not forgotten our nearest and dearest. But keeping in touch with loved ones is not the only motive for sending postcards. I heard of someone years ago who went on a luxurious, exotic holiday. They bought lots of postcards and in later years continued to send the foreign cards to their friends as if they had been on yet another expensive holiday. They did not fool anybody for very long as the stamp was obviously British! While this person may have been simply playing a practical joke, there may be some people who send cards to make other people envy them: 'Look at me, I've been on holiday to somewhere really special and you haven't.' And when they come back they either tell you how expensive and luxurious the experience was or else they boast about what a bargain it was. It's amusing hearing children in the playground arguing the relative merits of Disneyland Paris and Centerparcs but when adults compete in the same sort of way it starts to get embarrassing.

Today's reading on envy may speak to us here. In the first instance, it may be more directed at those who have not been able to go on holiday, perhaps not in some years. It is a warning against envy. We might think that life is not fair and that other people do not deserve the holiday they have had as much as we do, although we could not afford one. But there is nothing in principle against visiting other places in order to have a refreshing change. Nor is there anything wrong in principle in telling other people about it. However, at the very least it would be the height of insensitivity to boast about a cruise around the Mediterranean to an unemployed family who have not been able to have more than the odd visit to relations during the past few years.

To those who have been fortunate to go away somewhere special for a holiday, the message is this: by all means enjoy yourselves, but please be careful to avoid boasting about it. To those who have not been so fortunate, the message is this: do not envy those who have been on holiday, even if you think that they did not deserve it. Envy won't make any difference to them and will not do you any good.

Today's reading also offers us some consolation: if we continue in our relationship with God ('in the fear of the Lord') then we shall be forward-looking and confident that our future is secure with him. Our focus should be on God, not on what other people have or haven't done on holiday. In that way we may gladden God's heart.

Prayer

Dear Lord, the source of every blessing and of everything good that happens, we thank you for time off, holidays and the people we can share the experience with. Help us to be sensitive to those who do not enjoy time off, either because they do not have any or because it brings no relief from their worries. Help everyone we know to come to realize that within your presence is enjoyment and that no circumstances can separate us from you. Protect us, and all those whom we love, from envy and boasting. In the name of Jesus Christ. Amen

Drunkenness

PROVERBS 23:19–21

Hear, my child and be wise, and direct your mind in the way. Do not be among the winebibbers, or among gluttonous eaters of meat; for the drunkard and the glutton will come to poverty, and drowsiness will clothe them with rags.

PROVERBS 23:29–35

Who has woe? Who has sorrow? Who has strife? Who has complaining? Who has wounds without cause? Who has redness of eyes? Those who linger late over wine, those who keep trying mixed wines. Do not look at wine when it is red, when it sparkles in the cup and goes down smoothly. At the last it bites like a serpent, and stings like an adder. Your eyes will see strange things, and your mind utter perverse things. You will be like the one who lies down in the midst of the sea, like the one who lies on the top of a mast. 'They struck me,' you will say, 'but I was not hurt; they beat me, but I did not feel it. When shall I awake? I need another drink.' (v. 35d—GNB)

These two passages from the same chapter share a similar theme. They offer useful insights and may well be informed by some personal experiences of drinking too much alcohol!

The first few verses surely reflect a concern of all responsible parents and guardians. A frequent worry for them is the company that their children keep. As children grow up, there are times when allowing them to start taking their own decisions brings special anguish, when they seem to be deliberately choosing a peer group that does not fit their parents' values or standards. Here is a plea from such a parent to their child: avoid drinkers and those who stuff themselves with food. It may be that the 'winebibbers' and 'gluttons' are contemporaries of the child or they may be older, but their lifestyle is to be avoided whatever other attractions their friendship might hold.

This is not a plea for either teetotalism or for vegetarianism. In the first instance, it is a straightforward warning against waste. If you habitually drink and eat more than you need, then your stocks of food are going to decrease more rapidly than usual, and if you spend all your time eating and drinking or partying, how will you have enough time to stock up again? These are some of the questions implied here.

Secondly, it is about being fit and healthy. If you are half asleep, hung over or simply lethargic from eating so much food, then you are not going to achieve much. How will you earn a living? The implied answer is that you will not. Instead you will end up poor, dressed in rags through being unable to afford new clothes.

Of course, such a person may be too drowsy to notice!

Although there is a serious message behind it, I have to confess that I find the second passage rather amusing. Try reading it out loud to see what I mean.

I think this brilliant passage must have been penned from bitter experience, close observation, or both. There is a very effective comparison between drunkenness and seasickness: the swaying motion, the nausea. Then there is the hangover, the 'morning after the night before' when the memory of getting drunk is hazy at best. There is the pounding headache: 'Did I fall over? I must have been hit over the head for it to hurt so bad.' Perhaps the drunk imagines someone must have been beating him but cannot find the bruises, although the aches and pains are there. Perhaps he got into a fight but he cannot remember. Finally, true to form, he fumbles after more alcohol in the vain hope that it will make things better.

And there is the darker side of drunkenness—not mentioned here, but all too familiar—the loud talking, threatening or dangerous behaviour, violence, drunken driving, fighting, loss of control, accidents, death.

The perils of gluttony and drunkenness are mentioned several times in the Bible. In a society where there was no social security, the personal financial crisis envisaged by our proverbs would have been much more acute than for us today. Yet the personal tragedy is just as bad. As well as domestic problems some of the consequences can be clearly seen on far too many streets in our communities. Naturally we should have ways of helping those fellow citizens but the advice here to our children is never to go down that path in the first place.

To consider

1. Given the drawbacks of drinking alcohol, should Christians be teetotal?
2. To what extent is the advice for children in today's first reading realistic?

The practical application of today's reading is straightforward: don't get drunk!

Prayer

Lord God, thank you for all the good things you give us to eat and drink. We pray for those for whom food is a master, not a servant; or where drink is a demon, not a blessing. Grant them and us your Spirit and the gifts of moderation and self-control. Amen

Adultery

PROVERBS 23:26–28

My child, give me your heart, and let your eyes observe my ways. For a prostitute is a deep pit; an adulteress is a narrow well. She lies in wait like a robber and increases the number of the faithless.

Here is an example of proverbial training. In the Hebrew, the word translated 'child' is in fact 'son'. It has the feel of a father using a graphic image to make a point to his son. The strength of the images reveals something of the strength of feeling behind the instruction. The principles expounded here, though, apply equally to both sexes, even if the exact form of words reflects ancient Hebrew society more closely than our own.

The first thing we might notice is that the parent says, 'Look at my example.' Here is someone who is *not* saying, 'Do as I say, not as I do.' If we take this at face value, then we can believe that this person is not a hypocrite and does actually practise what he preaches. That example, in the end, is more likely to have an effect than the actual details of the advice given.

It seems unfair to single out the prostitute for condemnation and not the people who use her. The clients and those who make money out of the whole sordid business bear just as much moral responsibility. Actually, the Bible does condemn those hypocrites who decry society's lack of moral fibre while they themselves are in fact adulterous (see, for example, 2 Samuel 11—12 and Genesis 38). The issue is not about those who fall into prostitution out of a desperate attempt to provide for their family. It would be better in those cases to regard them more as victims than criminals. Indeed, Genesis 38 tells a curious story in which a woman prostitutes herself as a desperate measure to get her rights. The man, an important public figure, condemns the very woman he has had sex with. She is in danger of losing her life until the man is caught out and the woman's rights and reputation are restored.

The issue here is that there are some people who have made it their profession to prey on human weakness—and prostitutes are not the only ones for that matter, for there is the whole business of pornography which is contrary to the moral teaching of the Bible. Sex outside marriage does not help the family or strengthen relations within it.

Somehow the belief has arisen that sex is dirty, some kind of necessary evil that religious people try to avoid. Perhaps this has come about because some people are admired for their special calling to celibacy and the assumption that it is the superior way of getting close to God. But it is not true that sex is dirty or inferior. As well as being pleasurable, sex is holy—after all, God invented it—and it matters very much how you share your body in that intimate way.

In today's passage, the parent uses a stark image about the prostitute (who gives sex for payment) and the adulteress (who has betrayed her husband). Both are described as a trap—one from which it is hard to escape. To fall in with either of them is costly not just in terms of money or gifts handed over but in terms of the loss of trust and respect. At the heart of the matter is not whether sex is good or bad, but whether or not we value faithfulness in relationships. Prostitution and adultery are wrong not because sex is dirty but because unfaithfulness damages relationships and can even destroy them. The practical advice here is not about how to juggle the relationships with your lover and your spouse—the advice is to make them one and the same person.

Prayer

Almighty God, creator of all that is good, holy and fun, have mercy on us who are tempted to be unfaithful in any way. Heal broken relationships and restore those who truly repent. Amen

Week Five

Honesty

Proverbs 24:26
One who gives an honest answer gives a kiss on the lips.

'Honesty is the best policy' and 'Do not tell lies' are alternative, though less poetic, ways of saying much the same thing. It should come as no surprise to us that the God of all wisdom, all knowledge and all truth should be in favour of honest conduct and of telling the truth. Fundamental to any code of conduct, whether a religious one or not, are the principles of truth and rightness. The whole point of the code is to be able to know what is right—at least in the eyes of whoever drew up that code. Without honesty, we naturally end up with lies which build up to contradict and cancel each other out. The result is that we find we can never be sure of anything. In the end, lies gain us nothing.

As well as being pragmatic, truth is valuable in its own right. The 'kiss on the lips' is a sign of true friendship. One of the words used in the New Testament for worshipping God can be translated something like 'blowing a kiss' (for example, in Hebrews 1:6; Revelation 4:10 and 11:1, which refer specifically to angelic worship in heaven). The idea conveys both respect and affection—by it we are honouring someone whom we not only admire but also love. And a kiss has romantic connotations as well. A whole range of emotions can be bound up with that 'first kiss': excitement, uncertainty, fear, panic, joy or even revulsion. It can mark the turning point of a relationship as a couple embarks on an exploration of a deeper level of relationship. A kiss can also symbolize a bond between members of a family.

Although a kiss may well be a sign of true friendship, it can be used to tell a lie itself. When Judas betrayed Jesus he did so as he gave him a kiss of true friendship and hailed him as 'Master'.

Imagine one of your friends arriving with a gang of thugs, saying, 'You're my best friend!' just as they take you away to beat you up.

Let's not dwell on Judas' lie. Let's go back to today's saying and consider what that 'true friendship' means in practice. One way of showing true friendship is by giving an honest answer. I am sure that none of us ever sets out to lie to our friends and probably rarely does so. But aren't there ever times we find ourselves hesitating at some of the questions they ask us? Sometimes, perhaps without fully realizing it, we try to work out what they want us to say. Sometimes we avoid criticizing them when really we ought to. Sometimes we tell ourselves that we are being tactful when what we are actually doing is avoiding the issue. There is nothing wrong with carefully choosing our words and the time and place for saying something—if we can. Yet holding back from the truth may not always be the most loving thing to do. If we love someone, there are times when we do have to risk upsetting them (no matter how much we want to avoid that) in order to tell them something important.

One thing we should note about today's proverb is that it is about an honest answer. The implication is that the other person has asked us a question. We are not being encouraged to go around telling our friends unpleasant home truths. Criticizing other people when our opinion has not been sought is generally unhelpful. Part of loving is exercising patience with other people and with their faults. That can often mean keeping our mouths tightly shut when we want to complain. Perhaps the proverb might be more helpful to us if it began 'If asked, one who gives an honest answer...'

Honesty is the best policy, not just because it means we won't get caught out, but because it is the most loving thing to do. At the end of the day, an honest answer humbly given is a sign of true friendship.

To consider

1. What would happen if we all spoke honestly all the time?
2. Why might there be times when it is right to be dishonest?
3. How should we react if someone tells us an unpleasant truth?

Prayer

Almighty Father, give us the courage to be honest with our friends, the wisdom to do it tactfully and the grace to speak out of love. Amen

Humility

PROVERBS 25:6–7

Do not put yourself forward in the king's presence or stand in the place of the great; for it is better to be told, 'Come up here,' than to be put lower in the presence of a noble.

I am sure Jesus had these verses in mind when he said, 'For all who exalt themselves will be humbled, and those who humble themselves will be exalted' (Luke 14:11). At one level these verses are about etiquette. It is not the done thing to grab the best place for yourself, so at least put on a show of humility. On a straightforward, pragmatic level, when we are at some formal occasion and have the slightest doubt where we should go, then our best tactic is to take the least important place—a corner table, say, not the top table. That way, if we are not so important, then at least we have got somewhere to sit. If, in fact, the important person, the host, wants us higher up, then we will be promoted to a better place—with the advantage of being seen by everyone else as a favourite of the host. In short, it is better to start low and get promoted than to start high up and be demoted publicly. By following the advice of this saying, we can avoid social embarrassment, if nothing else!

Yet Jesus tells such a story (Luke 14:7–10) with a deeper message behind it. One of his key kingdom values is meekness, and Jesus is at pains to convey this idea not just in words but in actions too. He mentions it in the Sermon on the Mount (Matthew 5) and demonstrates it by doing the slave's task of washing his disciples' feet (John 13). Despite what we might assume, meekness is not weakness. In fact, to be truly meek requires strength and confidence. Meek people know their place and are confident of their status: they are loved by God as his children and know that they are co-heirs with Christ. What more could they want? They do not need to push or shove. They do not need to make a fuss or grab what they think they deserve.

Christians sometimes confuse meekness with false humility. I once arrived at a house for a meeting at about the same time as one other person. We were the last two. In the room there were two spare seats. One was a hard and straight-backed chair; the other was a comfortable armchair. We both hesitated and then, like good Christians, we both insisted that the other have the better chair. After about five minutes of intense dialogue I gave in and sat down in the comfortable chair, leaving my companion with the satisfaction of showing how much more humble he was as he took the harder chair. What a waste of time! Although superficially we were trying to keep to the Bible's teaching on meekness, we actually ended up competing with each other to show how 'Christian' we were. It was anything but humble.

Another more serious misunderstanding about humility and meekness concerns our own needs. We are taught to put the needs of others before our own—that is a key Christian value. But that is not the same as pretending that we do not have needs of our own. To do so is just another kind of pride.

A trivial example of this happened at another house group meeting. The host offered tea or coffee. Instead of asking for what they wanted, each guest tried to guess what everyone else was going to have in order 'not to be any trouble'. The first person asked for coffee. The second, not liking coffee but not wanting to be any trouble, also asked for coffee. The third person could not drink coffee so asked for tea. The fourth, seeing that both were available, also asked for tea. At this point, the second person realized that tea would be available, changed their mind and asked for tea instead. The first person was now outnumbered and although they would rather have had coffee, asked for tea instead because they did not want to be any trouble. Unfortunately the fifth person just could not stand tea so asked for coffee. By this time, the host was getting a bit fed up and stated that both tea and coffee were on offer so would people please make up their minds! In trying 'not to be any trouble', and as a result not being honest about what they really wanted, the guests were being anything but humble.

Part of being humble may well be to accept uncomfortable circumstances without grumbling. But it is no part of humility to be dishonest about our needs. Having acknowledged what we really need, it may still be necessary to have those needs unmet because we are considering the needs of others first. On yet another home meeting occasion, someone arrived and saw that the only chair left was the armchair. He had the honesty and the humility to own up to the fact that, because of a back problem, he actually needed a hard, straight-backed chair. Someone gladly gave up their seat for that person.

The wisdom of today's saying is more subtle and more profound than showing other people how important or how holy we are. The key is to combine honesty about our needs with humility in a strength of character that has nothing to prove.

To consider

1. How can you tell when meekness means holding back and when it requires us to step forward?
2. In what other ways might people think they are showing humility when in fact all that they are doing is drawing attention to themselves? Do any of them apply personally?
3. How could today's proverb be useful at the next party you go to?

Prayer

Almighty God, give us confidence in our relationship with you through Jesus Christ, so that we may serve you and the people around us with true love, honesty and humility. Amen

WEEK 5 DAY 3

Revenge

PROVERBS 25:21–22

If your enemies are hungry, give them bread to eat; and if they are thirsty, give them water to drink; for you will heap coals of fire on their heads, and the Lord will reward you.

ROMANS 12:21

Do not be overcome by evil, but overcome evil with good.

The verse from Paul's letter to the Romans is included because Paul quotes this proverb in verse 20 of chapter 12. It is a chapter that describes the character of the Christian life in the light of the gospel of what God has done for us in the life, death and resurrection of Jesus Christ. Paul spends a considerable amount of space explaining that the Old Testament Law, while good, was not able to save us from sins and death. In fact, in his view the Law was worse than useless because we could never keep it all the time and it simply highlighted the fact of how much we were enslaved to sin. Nevertheless, he thanks God that we have been rescued by Jesus Christ from our predicament of a broken relationship with the heavenly Father. Then he goes back to those very Old Testament scriptures and quotes from them! What he is saying is that holy living will not earn us a place in heaven—but because of Jesus we do have our home there and so we ought to dedicate ourselves to leading a holy life. In today's reading we have an example of the sort of thing Paul had in mind.

Jesus also taught, 'Love your enemies' (Matthew 5:44; Luke 6:35) and here we have a practical instance of what that might entail. 'Love' here is not the emotional feeling but the attitude and action of love. This love does good despite what it may feel. It is not immediately obvious whether the 'enemy' refers to a foreign country at war with our own or to a personal enemy nearby. I think it is the latter, but I do not see why the principle should not be applied internationally too.

Are we being invited to delight in other people's misfortune? I do not think so. But what about our enemies, those people intent on harming us? No, not even theirs. If our enemies are in desperate need, they are human beings in desperate need, and as such they should be helped. Maybe the burning coals refer to red-hot faces of embarrassment and humiliation—maybe that loss of face for them is the sweeter revenge for us. I do not know. Both Proverbs and Romans go on. Proverbs continues, '... and the Lord will reward you' while in Romans it says, 'Do not be overcome by evil, but overcome evil with good'. In other words, this course of action is not only for our benefit but has a wider significance.

The real victory is not in defeating our enemies, because the real enemy is evil itself. As soon as we start fighting in the conventional sense, whether with fists, guns, bombs or words, then evil has already won. This is regardless of the outcome of the battle, for even the victor has lost to evil. The principle here is that it is possible and far preferable to overcome evil with good. Imagine two enemies trying to win by outdoing each other in acts of kindness. Regardless of who comes out on top, they are both winners and will probably end up as friends. Even if they do not, at least good may triumph.

Today's proverb complements Proverbs 21:22 (Week 3 Day 7 in this book). It may sound unrealistically idealistic, but in all this is the principle that our priorities must be about good overcoming evil.

To consider

1. How might it be possible to transfer the principle of today's proverb to disputes between countries?
2. Apart from giving food and drink, what other acts of kindness could be included here?

Prayer

Almighty Father, creator and rescuer of all peoples in every nation, forgive us our hatreds and enmities. Give us the grace and courage to overcome evil with good; in the name of Jesus Christ, our Saviour. Amen

Words

PROVERBS 26:2

Curses cannot hurt you unless you deserve them. They are like birds that fly by and never settle (GNB).

I remember being taught that 'sticks and stones may break your bones but words can never harm you'. I did not believe it. Words can wound even when the comment is unfair, untrue or undeserved. I am inclined not to believe today's proverb either. After all, if anyone were to tell lies about me in public, it would make me fearful of my reputation and would certainly make me feel bad. Criticism, even in private from a loved one, makes me want to retaliate in kind.

Yet the truth of this saying is not about feelings. Nor is it about lies as such, although they may be included. The key idea concerns curses. Curses convey evil intent and are the opposite of blessings. We might think of a 'spiritual curse' as something like a spell or a 'hex'. Equally we could think of a stream of invective and abuse from the mouth of a mad or angry person. For example, a man swaying with the effect of alcohol tried to board a coach for which he had no ticket. The conductor explained that not only was there a company rule about not carrying people who are 'the worse for drink' but the seats were all taken and safety regulations did not permit any more passengers. The conductor was courteous while explaining this. The would-be passenger vented his frustration by swearing, cursing and hurling abuse at the conductor. To his credit, the conductor did not turn a hair. He knew that he was in the right and that he did not deserve the curses. He realized that the other man was simply letting off steam, even if it was in a rather anti-social manner. If I had been that conductor I would have been sorely tempted to feel bad, be offended, feel threatened, even. I might indeed forget that I did not actually deserve the curses.

One example that Christians look to is that of Jesus when he had been arrested. The Gospels differ in the precise details of the events leading up to his crucifixion. They do not agree precisely as to who interrogated him or in what order the questioning came. We cannot be exactly sure what questions were asked of him. Yet all describe Jesus as refusing to respond to taunts or insults. In fact, all the Gospels remark upon his not retaliating. It would appear from the Gospels that, by the time he had been arrested, nothing he said was going to make a difference to what would happen to him. Yet not only did he refuse to plead for his life or respond to the insults that were hurled at him, but he did not curse or swear at all as far as we can tell. For Christians Jesus' restraint in such circumstances is an example to emulate but hard to equal.

In today's saying, it is pointed out that undeserved curses are like a flock of birds—however many there are, they are just flying by. We do not have to catch them or encourage them to build a nest. It may take some determination and repeated effort to get out of the habit of taking everything to heart, including undeserved comments. It requires us to be honest and patient with ourselves. We need to learn to ignore the invective. We also need to be honest enough to recognize when we have done something wrong and deserve to be reprimanded. Either way, we should do our best not to give landing rights to the birds!

Prayer

Lord of all creation, by your word everything comes into being and through words your gospel is proclaimed to the world. Let us not abuse the power of the word or be harmed by it. May all our words and our lives serve your glory and reveal your love in the world. Amen

Gossip

PROVERBS 26:20
Without wood, a fire goes out; without gossip, quarrelling stops (GNB).

I suppose it should be painfully obvious what this saying means. The point is made using a fairly familiar image. If we have ever made a camp fire or a bonfire, we should easily recognize the fact that a fire needs material to burn and if we run out of material then the fire goes out. Today's proverb provides us with an opportunity to consider what material keeps quarrelling going.

Telling tales, spreading rumours—whether true or not—is well known to cause or continue quarrels and arguments. Half-truths can sometimes be the most damaging because most people tend to think, 'There's no smoke without fire' and assume the worst based on what they have heard. There is an equivalent saying to our proverb: 'Least said, soonest mended'. In other words, whatever the cause of the argument, the sooner the matter can be left alone, the sooner the positive work of reconciliation can take place.

Once an apology has been made and accepted—or even simply an agreement concluded as a truce—then that should be the end of the matter. We may be tempted to make either repeated apologies or long-winded explanations, which are really just thinly disguised attempts at justifying ourselves. It is possible to apologize so much that the argument starts all over again! One useful strategy is to develop a good 'forgetory' (the opposite of memory!) This means deciding to avoid talking about the wrong subject by deliberately choosing to concentrate on something else instead.

There is, of course, the real danger of leaving truly important issues unresolved. The proverb makes two main points in relation to this question. First, it is chiefly concerned with gossip, reminding us to 'mind our own business', no matter how interesting the rumours may seem.

Second, even if the issue concerned is of real importance, quarrelling about it will not help. In that situation, time out to let emotions cool down may be the best next step. Yet when it comes to talking the matter through, we would be dishonest to deny the strong feelings we have and we may have to explain why the matter is so important to us. Of course, it is not wrong to have strong emotions, nor is it wrong to let them indicate to us how important something really is, as far as we are concerned. But such strong feelings are not very good at helping us think things through and can even get in the way of learning something of value from the person with whom we are disagreeing.

The New Testament has two maxims we could usefully put alongside today's saying. Both are from Paul's letters. The first is 'As far as possible live in peace with one another' (Romans 12:18, paraphrase). That includes trying not to get into unnecessary arguments in the first place and making it our habit not to gossip or pass on rumours. The other is 'Do not let the sun go down on your anger' (Ephesians 4:26). Not only will that help us to sleep better but it will help us not to accumulate bad feelings day by day. We may have to sort out the trouble on the very day that it occurs. It may simply mean deciding to forgive someone before they have had the opportunity to apologize. It is not a virtue to harbour grudges. At the heart of the Christian gospel is forgiveness and putting that into practice will also help to avoid quarrelling.

Perhaps we can best express the meaning of today's proverb like this: 'Forgive and forget' and 'Mind your own business'.

Prayer

Heavenly Father, set a guard over our lips to help us watch what we say. Give us kind hearts and kind words. Help us to learn when to shut up and when to apologize. Amen

Hidden love

PROVERBS 27:5
Better is open rebuke than hidden love.

How can being horrible to someone be good? After all, being rude about other people is not very kind, is it? My first reaction to this saying was to wonder if we are really being asked to go round telling people off!

One day, I actually did discover what the proverb was getting at when I faced a dilemma. I cannot remember whether it was at home or work, but I do recall that it involved someone close to me being seriously in the wrong. I knew it but they did not. I did not want an argument and I did not want to hurt or offend them. Should I say anything to them and if so, what? I did wonder whether the most loving course of action was to keep quiet but try to encourage them in what they actually did get right.

The 'hidden love' mentioned here could mean one of two things. It could mean an unspoken compliment or word of encouragement, which could boost someone's morale and help them do something even better than before. Perhaps it means a declaration of love like announcing to someone for the first time, 'I love you.' Alternatively, the 'hidden love' might be the holding back of correction or necessary criticism. When we are looking after children we may be tempted to think that ignoring bad behaviour is the same as loving them, but it is no way of teaching them to learn right from wrong.

The main concern for this verse, however, is that refusing to express deserved criticism is unhealthy and unhelpful. Sometimes it may be kinder in the long run to hold back from an intended compliment to make a necessary criticism. If our teachers had never corrected us at school we would hardly have learnt anything.

The principle here is that as we strive to be loving in all we do and say, we must also be honest. Of course that does not mean we have to point out every mistake a loved one makes. It does mean, however, that sometimes the most loving action can seem painful in the short term.

Another translation (GNB) puts it this way: 'Better to correct someone openly than to let him think you don't care for him at all'. That gets to the heart of the matter: all of this is in order to show how much we care for our friends and is a maxim for any friendship that we cherish at all.

Sometimes it seems that we have to choose between loyalty to our friends and doing what we know to be right. In that case we have to ask ourselves if we are truly being loyal if we let them carry on doing wrong and say nothing. And we might wonder if they are really our friend if they treat us in the same way.

To consider

1. What sorts of things do you let your family and friends get away with?
2. What do they let you get away with?
3. How should we tackle a friend or colleague whom we discover doing something illegal or immoral?

Prayer

Lord God, guard our words and our actions. Prompt us to speak out both to encourage and to correct those near us. Give us the true friendship that is both kind and honest in every situation. Amen

Danger

PROVERBS 27:12

The clever see danger and hide; but the simple go on, and suffer for it.

Cowards of the world, unite! At first glance this proverb is very much of the 'discretion is the better part of valour' type, but there are times when we need to face danger and take risks for the sake of the love of God and our neighbour. In this country we are very fortunate to have so many dedicated people in the emergency services, regularly putting themselves at risk to save lives. Not only that, we rely on people taking risks to provide us with all kinds of commodities, whether they come from down a mine or out at sea. Yet today's saying seems to imply that clever people are those cowards who hide from danger and that it is simple, stupid people who face danger and endure the suffering that follows. In fact, this saying is not about carefully calculated action intended to help other people. In a nutshell it can be interpreted like this: 'Clever people take precautions, stupid people take unnecessary risks.'

We know the sort of thing. Come winter, a local pond, lake or river may be frozen over. The clever think, 'Danger—could be thin ice' and will not consider going near it unless they know it is safe. The stupid are on the ice in a moment, rushing to have a go at skating. If they have not ventured too far they might just get their feet wet in freezing water. At worst, the ice may give way in the middle and the deep, freezing water claims another fatality.

A similar rule applies when at the seaside where there are warnings about strong currents. Around the British coast there are many exciting places to visit with dramatic views or fascinating wildlife to watch. In one such place, on the east coast of England, low tide reveals a vast expanse of sand, and the sea goes so far out that it is possible to visit dunes and islands on foot that usually are inaccessible. Channels that are treacherous at high tide become streams, less than knee deep. In places you can step right over them. At one point, the low tide allows a short-cut of a few yards which avoids a walk of nearly four miles along a peninsular when the tide is in. It is quite common for someone to cross the stream at low tide to explore the dunes on the other side, only to discover a fast-flowing torrent blocking their way when they try to return. Many a visitor is caught out that way each year because they did not take the trouble to check the tide table.

One year, a man took his three-year-old child across the stream and with great delight they were both able to jump across it in one leap. They then set about exploring the dunes, playing in the sand and hoping for a glimpse of a seal or two. Unfortunately, when they came to return, the man discovered that he had misjudged the time slightly and the tide was already coming in. He did not want to walk the extra four miles, and he saw that they could not jump over the stream any more, but the man reckoned he could wade through it, carrying his child on his shoulders. As they came down the beach, people on the other side started waving and shouting at him. At first he thought they were urging him to hurry but he quickly realized that they were calling out things like 'Don't do it!' 'Turn back, the tide is very fast and the currents are dangerous'; 'Go the long way, now. You haven't got enough time' and so on. The man took no notice, picked the child up on to his shoulders and started into the water. In the time it took them to reach the water's edge, the river had risen from waist- to chest-deep. Still the people cried out from the opposite bank, 'Go back!' As the man felt the relentless force of the water and realized that it would be impossible to get across even if he were a strong swimmer, he turned back and struggled up on to the bank. By the time they reached the top, the channel was close behind and the swirling water brought it home to the man what a near miss he had had. He had wanted to cut a few miles and had nearly lost their lives instead. When they saw the man turn round and climb back up the bank, the people cheered and breathed a big sigh of relief.

As a rule, the wise thing to do is to avoid danger if we can and to minimize the risks if we cannot. The stupid thing is to carry on regardless of the circumstances and heedless of the consequences. It is not inherently wrong to take risks—sometimes it is necessary. But it is wrong to be careless or irresponsible. Clever people do not have to say, 'Whoops, sorry!' or cry for help nearly as much as the heedless do.

Underlying this saying is the question, 'Do you care about the consequences of your actions?' Other people are affected by what we do. If we care about them, then we try not to hurt them. If we do not take care, we end up hurting others without intending to because we just did not think. Most years there are reports of tragedies where someone has ignored danger signs.

The principle of this proverb applies all the year round, of course. There is perhaps a temptation to take more risks on holiday. It is good to try out new experiences but just because we happen to be on holiday it does not mean we should take unnecessary risks or ignore the safety precautions the experts on the field advise us to take.

To consider

1. What safety instructions do you regularly ignore?
2. In what ways is it possible to take too many precautions?
3. How do we decide what risks are acceptable?

Prayer

Eternal Father, thank you for giving us a wonderful and exciting universe. Thank you for everyone and everything that makes it so interesting and enjoyable. Let everyone have fun without hurting anyone and let us hear good advice and follow it. Amen

Week Six

Sharpening wits

PROVERBS 27:17
Iron sharpens iron, and one person sharpens the wits of another.

Why do we send children to school or students to college? Surely these days you can learn from television and a computer what you cannot get from books? In some respects this is true. There are millions of facts and bits of information that we can acquire outside school and college by way of libraries and the Internet. But there are social reasons why solitary learning is not enough. Many people think it important for children to mix with others of their age, partly to enjoy their childhood together, partly to learn how to get on with different people. Perhaps less crucial, but still important, is the need for students to mix with different people either from other backgrounds or from different places, including other countries. Although distance learning courses provide study opportunities for those who cannot go away to learn, they often provide some contact with tutors or fellow students—at a summer school, perhaps.

Apart from the social side, the opportunity for people to learn from each other is equally important. A teacher can tell whether a pupil really has understood a lesson by asking him or her to explain it or even teach it to a fellow pupil. Some of the best-learnt lessons are the ones where the learners have discovered the facts for themselves, often after some early disagreement and argument.

However young or old, rich or poor, busy or leisurely we may be, there is always something to learn, and we can learn a lot from the people around us. We should value the conversations we have with our friends, family and colleagues. They may sharpen our wits, as the proverb states, and help us to understand what we think we already know. Of course, it is possible to learn by ourselves but we often come to understand a lot better by talking things through with others.

The popular stereotype of a wise man is of someone who lives alone on a mountain, spending all day deep in meditation. People come from hundreds of miles around to seek his advice and take back with them his wise sayings. In one sense, the book of Proverbs is presented as a collection of sayings from such wise people or gurus, yet today's saying contradicts the idea that wisdom can only be found in such an esoteric way. It is not to say that spending time alone without distractions is unhelpful—people go on retreat for that very reason and spend time in silence. What today's proverb says is that wisdom can be found in the company of other people.

In the early centuries of Christianity, some people went to live in the desert because they felt that it was difficult to be close to God amid the distractions of everyday life. Eventually people started to visit them in search of wise counsel. After a while, though, the desert dwellers found it difficult to live alone without being in danger of losing touch with reality, or of simply getting strange ideas with no one to talk them through with! So they came together to form basic Christian communities with a simple lifestyle, dedicated to Christian fellowship and a life of prayer. It was out of these fellowships that monasteries and similar communities came into being. These much-respected people had discovered that they needed other people too.

Whatever kind of learning we do, whatever kind of prayer life we have, whatever time by ourselves we have, it is important to value the opinions of others and to spend some of our time with other people. One example of this is in our prayer life. We can and should spend some time alone with God in prayer. Equally, too, we should worship with others as well as learning from them. It is not as if there is a law that says we must go to church. Rather, we need to remember that if we are to grow as Christians, we need to worship together. We need other Christians to keep us sharp.

Prayer

Lord God, source of all wisdom and understanding, thank you for the people with whom we can talk things over. Help us to sharpen our wits in order to love, understand and serve you more effectively.
Amen

Flattery

PROVERBS 29:5
Whoever flatters a neighbour is spreading a net for his feet (NIV).

So what is wrong with flattery, may I ask? Surely there is nothing wrong with a few compliments now and again. It feels good to be told something positive about ourselves, does it not? I certainly much prefer people to say nice things about me than to hear them tell me something negative about myself. And what is all this about a net? Flattery has not got much to do with hunting or fishing, I am sure.

This saying is ambiguous. When it says 'his feet', whose does it mean? The NRSV translates it as 'the neighbour's feet'; the GNB translates it another way, so that it is the flatterer's own feet we are looking at. Perhaps it is deliberately ambiguous.

Perhaps we should take a closer look at the flatterer. First, this person is not just someone who is being kind or encouraging. The Hebrew word literally means someone who is smooth with his or her words. The flatterer's chief concern is not with how truthful they are being or how fair—whatever words are used, they are intended to make the hearer well disposed to the flatterer. Behind all the smooth talk is the intention to manipulate. This flatterer may think that the cause is worthwhile; indeed it may or may not be a selfish one. However, they are being deceitful, at least to their target if not to themselves. The deceit is in the fact that they are disguising their true intentions. And they can deceive themselves by saying that they are being 'diplomatic'.

The trap for the flatterer lies in the fact that they have used words to manoeuvre a more powerful or influential person to support their cause. Whether the cause is just or not, whether the comments are largely true or not, they have twisted the truth and used deceit. This deceit takes the flatterer several steps away from the truth, away from honesty and wisdom towards a trap of lies. Flattery is the beginning of a slippery slope—best not to take even one step along it.

I have had the mixed blessing of attending many meetings at church and at work, ranging from the business-like to the long and tedious. Some have been great fun, others fraught with controversy. I have heard people say something positive in order to soften the blow of some criticism they feel they have to make or to redress the balance of an otherwise negative meeting. I have left meetings tired and depressed. But I must tell you that the worst of the lot are the ones where someone has tried to use flattery to get their own way. You could say that watching someone butter up a group of people with the obvious intent of riding over their objections leaves a bad taste in the mouth. The manifest manipulation is worse than any actual decision taken. Fortunately such occasions are rare but the experience makes it very difficult to trust that person again. The flatterer not only risks the slippery slope which in the long run could lead to a tangle of lies but they also run the risk of being spotted for what they are and losing other people's trust and respect.

What about the neighbour? Where is the trap for him or her? It is nice to be flattered; it makes us feel important and good on the inside. It can be difficult to distinguish between genuine praise and manipulative flattery. The flatterer's intention is to make us open to suggestion—are we aware of what is going on? Flattery panders to our pride, and therein lies the trap. We start to hear what we want to hear; we find it harder and harder to hear critical voices. We may even begin to distrust our friends if they dare to express an honest opinion that we happen to dislike. We no longer see the world or ourselves as they really are. We end up seeing and hearing only what our flatterers show and tell us. We become trapped and, what is worse, we may not realize it.

We must not let a healthy mistrust of flattery get in the way of giving and receiving genuine compliments and encouragement, however. The principle expressed here is that we should not cynically use compliments to get our own way.

Prayer

God of hope, help us to discern the difference between truth and lies, praise and flattery, honesty and deceit. Thank you for our friends who are both loving and honest with us. Let us not fall into either trap of flattery; for you are our Lord and God of truth and love. Amen

Politics

PROVERBS 29:12–14

If a ruler listens to falsehood, all his officials will be wicked. The poor and the oppressor have this in common: the Lord gives light to the eyes of both. If a king judges the poor with equity, his throne will be established forever.

If I were the compiler of this little section, I think I would have put verse 13 first. The other two verses are about good government while this one is making the fundamental assertion on which the other two are based.

It is not obvious what lies behind the thought that God 'gives light to the eyes'. Perhaps it means that everyone who is able to see can do so by the same light shining around. There is not one sunlight for the poor and one for the rest. God is the ultimate source of all light: everyone ultimately depends on him in order to see. No one, then, can claim superiority, given that everyone depends on God.

Another way of understanding the 'light to the eyes' is as that sparkle we see in one another's eyes—the spark of life that does not depend on our status but on the fact that we are alive (although sometimes that sparkle is dimmed by ill health). The eyes have been thought to be a window into the soul and we can often understand something of the character of a person by looking into their eyes. When people habitually wear sunglasses, it is easy to imagine that they have something to hide. Thus the verse means that God is the source of that sparkle of life that you can sometimes see in people's faces and he gives it to all sorts of people in all walks of life.

Either way, verse 13 says that the poor and the oppressor have something in common. It does not say that they are the same or equal. In fact inequality is at the root of the situation being addressed. The poor are those who have less than enough, whether in terms of money or food or warmth or shelter, or all four. Inequality can also include lack of access to fundamental human rights: too few means of making a living, not enough influence on one's own situation, too little (if any) say when decisions are taken. The oppressor is anyone who exercises power in such a way that it disables other people, denying them power in any form whatsoever. The oppressor can be a national dictator, using violence or the threat of violence to subjugate his people, or a loan shark on a poor housing estate, making money out of other people's poverty by charging them interest that they really cannot afford.

What is not so obvious is that it is possible to be a nice person and yet be an oppressor. In fact, we could go so far as to say that there are plenty of well-intentioned people who are in effect oppressors. All it takes is an unfairly balanced trade agreement, a contract geared to protect the investment of money more than the individuals concerned, a legal system based on assumptions shared by only a fraction of society or a tax system weighted to attract large-scale investment rather than to relieve those stuck on a low income. In any of those instances, no matter how kind or generous we are as individuals, if we support or benefit from the unfair system then we are oppressors. We may honestly say, 'But it's not my fault. I didn't make the system' and we could be right. Maybe it is not our fault but we do now share some of the responsibility.

Nevertheless, although society and the 'system' may be unequal, God has no favourites based on social status.

All this means that those who do have power and influence must act wisely and justly, and this brings us to verses 12 and 14. An important skill for politicians is to be able to tell whether or not they are hearing the truth. It is a healthy sign when politicians show a real interest in discovering the truth of a matter, because when those in power take no notice of lies, they give the impression that they are more interested in holding on to power than in goodness. This makes it easier for wicked people to gain influence because the leaders have given tacit approval to deceit, which in turn breeds a culture of uncertainty, unhealthy competition and instability. And a politician's own position will be insecure if she or he is never sure how much the others are telling the truth.

Even where politicians make a priority of honesty and fairness, they will still have to work very hard and act courageously at times. Their future may even be more secure, although there is no guarantee of that. While they will treat everyone as if they matter, they will not be able to treat everyone exactly the same. Complete equality may have to wait for the after-life, but equity and fairness can be achieved in this one.

Today's verses have something for all of us to consider. Given the challenges facing politicians, it is all the more important that we should pray for them.

Prayer

Lord God, give our leaders, politicians and everyone in positions of power and influence your loving heart, fair minds and moral strength. In the name of Jesus Christ, your Son. Amen

Agur's wish

PROVERBS 30:7–9

Two things I ask of you; do not deny them to me before I die: Remove far from me falsehood and lying; give me neither poverty nor riches; feed me with the food that I need, or I shall be full, and deny you, and say, 'Who is the Lord?' or I shall be poor, and steal, and profane the name of my God.

Verse 8, 'Give me neither poverty nor riches', is sometimes referred to as 'Agur's wish' because chapter 30 records sayings attributed to Agur son of Jakeh. This particular phrase is one of those often quoted by some people without realizing its source. Some may even think it is an English saying, but as we can see, it is in the Bible. We do not know anything about Agur except for this mention in Proverbs.

There is a whole strand of teaching in Proverbs and many other books of the Bible which deals with injustice, the disparity of wealth, power, influence and safety in society. Here the issue is not about the social distribution of wealth, however. Here the issue is about the relationship between us and God.

I have no idea how old Agur was when he composed these sayings or when they were collected. Reading chapter 30 of Proverbs as a whole gives the impression of someone who has taken time and trouble to reflect on life experiences that have bothered, impressed or merely intrigued him. Some of the chapter is poetic advice, some simply says 'Look'. In any case, 'before I die' in verse 7 need not imply that Agur was particularly old but it does suggest a certain amount of impatience. The two things he asks for are important goals but he has not achieved them yet. Here is a person of integrity who wants neither to lie nor to be lied to. He has learnt that poverty and riches are both potential traps, and the stresses of being rich are not necessarily solved by becoming poor. And while poverty is not desirable, wealth brings its own problems.

Agur's wish, 'Give me neither poverty nor riches', leads us to the heart of the matter: whether we are rich or poor, what ultimately counts is our attitude. If we are greedy, it does not matter how much or how little we have—our greediness will not be affected either way. If we start off as poor and greedy and then grow rich, what is to stop us being rich and greedy? There will always be someone richer than we are. There will always be someone who has something we do not have. Perhaps we discover that envy is the problem and we decide to give everything away—but if we are still looking over the fence, wishing we owned what the neighbours own (even if now they are poor neighbours), then we have solved nothing.

All this is relevant to the most important relationship we can have: our relationship with God. If we know we are well off, we can be tempted to say, 'I need nothing more; no, not even God.' If we do not have enough to supply the needs of our family, we might justify stealing or some other crime. 'God has not helped us so we had better help ourselves' is the implicit thought here. It is hard to condemn someone who steals a loaf of bread in order to feed their starving family. The problem comes in knowing where to stop. Does this principle allow for stealing a television and video player in order to supply the need of a bored family? It is difficult to see how a life of crime honours God. Agur's wish is not just about getting the perfect balance of wealth and achieving the right lifestyle. It is about avoiding the kind of traps we have been discussing and about maintaining a right relationship with God.

God is not just there for the poor—he gives life to everyone, and everyone needs him. If we are poor, we might be inclined to blame God for our poverty and have nothing to do with him. If we are rich, we might just ignore him out of complacency. But God is not some kind of cosmic Santa Claus who doles out charity. Christians believe that the heart of a relationship with God is like that between a parent and child. Such a relationship involves more than just material concerns but includes love and virtue as well.

Whether we are rich or poor, we have to decide whether we want to succumb to either greed or envy. And, whatever our circumstances, it is up to us to decide how important our relationship with God is. We must remember, though, that we do not have forever to decide. Agur's 'before I die' is also 'before it is too late'.

Perhaps we should make 'Agur's wish' our own and pray that God will help us to have enough to live on and to learn to be content.

Prayer

Lord God, help me to realize when I have enough to live on. Let me never be complacent about the material blessings in my life, so that I may not ignore you; let me never use evil means to get what I need, so that I may not offend you. Protect me from evil and help me to resist greed and envy. Amen

Natural wonder

PROVERBS 30:18–19

Three things are too wonderful for me; four I do not understand: the way of an eagle in the sky, the way of a snake on a rock, the way of a ship on the high seas, and the way of a man with a girl.

More poetry than proverb, perhaps? For the romantic in me, this is one of my favourite Bible quotes. The first two phrases are a typical Hebrew literary device, perhaps designed as a memory aid when learning lists. There are other examples in chapter 30—see verses 15, 21 and 29.

Here we are introduced to three observations of movement in three 'dimensions': air, land and sea. I suppose the last line could be considered to refer to a fourth 'dimension' but of an altogether different kind. Perhaps the link is grace or beauty. Perhaps the observer wonders about the way they move. How can an eagle fly when it is heavier than air? How can a snake move even though it has no legs? Why does the ship sail, not sink? What moves people to fall in love?

For some people it is enough to pose the questions and marvel. For others comes the desire to pursue the answers to their questions. Close observation is the foundation of scientific curiosity, while the desire for universal answers makes for the beginnings of systematic enquiry. It is in such verses that we can see one point of contact between science and theology—a curiosity about the universe and wondering why things are as they are. Both science and theology look for answers and both scientists and theologians are capable of pride or narrow-mindedness, as well as being able to value truth, however surprising it may turn out to be. Whether scientist, theologian or both, there will always be occasions when we do not understand. Simply to stand and marvel at the beautiful and elaborate creation around us is a legitimate human activity.

So what is the practical application of these verses? Surely the point being made is that not every activity needs an immediate practical application. I remember talking with someone whom I much admired for his patience and prayerfulness. At one time he had been the Principal of a renowned theological college. He told me that he did not see the point in any theology that could not be put into practice. Theology as a purely academic exercise was a waste of time in his opinion. It is true that any academic study can be done without a real interest in the practical consequences. It is also true that you can do theology without a lively relationship with God and that studying theology can become a substitute for faith instead of its partner. In a similar way, pure research can appear to put scientists in an ivory tower. Too often it seems that we make advances in science before we have had time to consider properly the moral consequences of what has already been discovered. For both scientists and theologians, the danger is of being so absorbed in their work as to become out of touch with the needs and concerns of the rest of the world. And this can, of course, apply to anyone who gets wrapped up in their work.

Yet today's verse gives the other side of the story. It is good to be overwhelmed by wonder from time to time and you do not have to be a professional scientist or a professional theologian in order to be so.

Why not take some time just to spend looking around, maybe on a trip to the park or the countryside? Or you could look at the stars, or just watch the clouds float by. Whatever it is, spend some time enjoying the sight of something beautiful and thanking God for it.

Prayer

God of all time and space, creator of beauty and wisdom, we thank you for the marvels of your universe. Grant to all scientists and theologians integrity so that in the honest pursuit of their profession they may come ever closer to you; for you are truth and love. We ask this for the sake of your Son, Jesus Christ. Amen

Anger

PROVERBS 30:32–33

If you have been foolish, exalting yourself, or if you have been devising evil, put your hand on your mouth. For as pressing milk produces curds, and pressing the nose produces blood, so pressing anger produces strife.

How quaint: curds and whey—it sounds like a Victorian nursery rhyme. Alternatively, it is a basic recipe for making cheese. I remember at school, many years ago, I was shown how to make cheese with the sole ingredient being milk that had gone sour. The teacher had left a bottle of milk in the sunshine for a couple of days and then brought the bottle into the school and showed us how to make the cheese by straining off the whey and pressing the curds. While I am not sure if we actually ate any of the result, the lesson did go to show that cheesemaking is essentially a straightforward natural process.

Pressing the nose to produce blood, in verse 33, is simply offered as another example of natural cause and effect. Pressing the curdled milk produces curds; pressing a nose (presumably very hard!) produces blood. It is not surprising—and that is the point: the result is obvious to anyone with a gramme of sense or basic knowledge. This brings us to the end of today's saying: 'Pressing anger produces strife'. Just like the previous two examples, this statement is being offered as patently obvious. Apparently the Hebrew is subtler than our translations can easily show. There is a play on the words 'nose' and 'anger' so that the second phrase of verse 33 could read something like 'pressing anger produces bloodshed'. Perhaps we might put it like this: 'If you push someone too far, you may end up with a bloody nose!'

The warning of verse 33 is quite clear, but what does it mean in practice for us? We are in a situation where someone is angry and we have to decide what to do next. We could taunt them and make them even angrier. We could react with defensive anger ourselves. We could walk away. We could try to placate them. We might try to reconcile them to whomever or whatever has angered them. This saying does not tell us what to do exactly—there is no precise solution for coping with other people's anger. What it does give us is a basic principle: we should not deliberately provoke more trouble by provoking the angry person even further. For a moment, seeing someone in a rage might prove entertaining but someone could so easily get hurt—and that is wrong.

Another part of the answer has been given to us in verse 32. The main point here is not about us getting angry or wound up. It is about what we do or say that makes other people angry (or angrier if they are already mad). Some people are very easy to wind up. There are certain topics that you only have to mention and they get annoyed. Some things that other people joke about agitate them. Of course, we would never be so cruel as to make someone angry just for the sake of it, would we? So we might occasionally tease someone or pull their leg but that is not the same thing, is it? In fact, a lot of the time, one person's teasing is another person's provocation and we would be foolish not to realize that. We might think that 'winding someone up' is just harmless fun but if we were that person who is constantly provoked we could end up feeling quite stressed. It is not fair to pick on people even in the name of fun, and we should hardly be surprised if the reaction we get is anger. Go too far or too often and a punch (or worse) may follow.

If we are to grow wise, we need to stop and think from time to time what other people might actually be going through and be ready to bite our tongue if we are tempted to tease someone yet again.

Prayer
Loving God, our judge and our saviour, help us not to get angry. Give us grace not to stir up trouble and to know when to keep our mouths shut. Amen

What is wisdom?

PROVERBS 31:1, 4–6, 9

The words of King Lemuel. An oracle that his mother taught him... It is not for kings, O Lemuel, it is not for kings to drink wine, or for rulers to desire strong drink; or else they will drink and forget what has been decreed, and will pervert the rights of all the afflicted. Give strong drink to one who is perishing, and wine to those in bitter distress... Speak out, judge righteously, defend the rights of the poor and needy.

PROVERBS 31:29

Many women have done excellently, but you surpass them all.

Chapter 31 of Proverbs stands alone, almost like an afterthought. Verses 1–9 are attributed to Lemuel—or rather to his mother. Perhaps unfairly, I imagine an over-protective mother with a capable grown-up son who lives somewhat in her shadow. Of course she loves him and means well, but her presence looms rather large over him. This stereotype has been a boon to comedians but real life is usually more subtle and complex than that. There is nothing wrong with treasuring pearls of wisdom from our parents and, if we have found that they have lasting value, why not pass them on?

In the first half dozen verses or so, the basic message appears to be, 'My mother says I am too good for drink but it is OK for poor people.' With that rather crude simplification, we could then safely lump these verses with the other warnings on the subject. However, the reason given here for avoiding alcoholic drink is in order to keep a clear head, to rule wisely. Verses 8 and 9 contain an important message for any king or ruler and underline much of the justice theme that runs through the book.

In many ways, Proverbs can be seen as a handbook of practical wisdom for a would-be king or ruler, promoting the idea that the truly successful ruler will be wise and just. In particular, such a ruler will speak out for those who cannot speak for themselves and will pay particular attention to those who are powerless. Proverbs was written in a time that did not have democracy as we understand it and there were no extra votes for helping the poor. Yet rooted in the wisdom of the Bible is a 'bias to the poor' (it is not just a New Testament idea), not for the sake of political expediency but because it was believed that God is interested in everyone. In other words, King Lemuel's mother was right, not just clever.

The last verses of the book make up a poem about a capable wife. In terms of literary style it is quite cleverly crafted, although you cannot see it in English translation very easily. It has twenty-two verses, one for each letter of the Hebrew alphabet. Each verse begins with a different letter and they are all in the correct order. In English it might begin something like:

> *A capable wife is rare like jewellery,*
> *But her husband trusts her, doing well by her.*
> *Continually she does good, not harm.*
> *Diligently she works with her hands.*
> *Et cetera …*

On the face of it, this poem is a one-sided view of marriage: any husband who has a hardworking wife like this will make a profit and have a good place in society. To be fair, reading this poem on its own might tempt us to a sexist interpretation. It seems to put women in their place, running household affairs and being servants to their husbands—but that would be to miss the point.

I think that there are at least two main reasons for finding this poem here. First, let us consider how, in Proverbs, there are several occasions when an unfortunate picture of women is painted. A nagging wife is like a dripping tap—better to live on the roof. Meanwhile, beware the adulteress and temptress. While we should want to acknowledge the perils of adultery and temptation, in these days we also notice the negative association with women and the lack of the same kind of condemnation for men. This poem was not included out of our sense of equality. Perhaps, though, it was put here in the name of fairness and to redress the balance somewhat.

Second, though, Proverbs does portray wisdom as a feminine strength (see, for example, 1:20–21; 4:5–9)—a human quality that we ignore or undervalue at our peril—so maybe wisdom is the 'wife' referred to here and the poem describes the planning, hard work, perseverance and skill that a wise person demonstrates. Of course the picture in the poem reflects the kind of tasks a woman would be expected to carry out in ancient Israel, yet surely there is an enduring message we can take from this poem: be 'married' to wisdom. In other words, get acquainted with wisdom so that it guides everything we do.

The wisdom of the Bible is God-centred and acknowledges him as the source of all truth and knowledge. At its heart is both a relationship with him and also a concern with justice in society. Wisdom is no substitute for God but it can offer practical insights for putting his love into action in daily life, whatever our circumstances.

As we conclude this study of Proverbs, maybe now is a good point to stop and consider the state of our relationship with God. Ask him for wisdom to lead the kind of loving and just life that he wants for all of us.

Prayer

O Wisest Love, Creator and Redeemer, forgive our ignorance and destructive impulsiveness. Forgive the pride and arrogance that we confuse with truth and knowledge. Grant us the wisdom to be more faithful to you, more just in our society and more loving with all. Amen

Other publications from BRF

You may be interested in other publications from BRF. The following pages provide details of *New Daylight*, BRF's popular daily Bible reading notes, and two books by Margaret Cundiff.

For details of our full range of books for adults and children, write to:

BRF
Peter's Way
Sandy Lane West
Oxford
OX4 5HG

Tel: 01865 748227;
Fax: 01865 773150;
E-mail: enquiries@brf.org.uk

Alternatively, you may visit your local Christian bookshop.

New Daylight subscriptions

New Daylight is ideal for those looking for a fresh, devotional approach to reading and understanding the Bible. Each issue covers four months of daily Bible reading and reflection with each day offering a Bible passage (text included), helpful comment and a prayer or thought for the day ahead.

The notes are edited by David Winter, an Anglican priest in the Diocese of Oxford, former BBC Head of Religious Broadcasting at the BBC, and regular contributor to Thought for the Day and Prayer for Today. *New Daylight* is written by a gifted team of contributors including Adrian Plass, Brother Ramon, Hilary McDowell, Marcus Maxwell, Margaret Cundiff, Henry Wansbrough, Rosemary Green, Rob Gillion, Graham Dodds and Peter Graves.

New Daylight is also available in large print and on cassette for the visually impaired.

NEW DAYLIGHT SUBSCRIPTIONS

❑ I would like to give a gift subscription
(please complete both name and address sections below)
❑ I would like to take out a subscription myself
(complete name and address details only once)

This completed coupon should be sent with appropriate payment to BRF. Alternatively, please write to us quoting your name, address, the subscription you would like for either yourself or a friend (with their name and address), the start date and credit card number, expiry date and signature if paying by credit card.

Gift subscription name _____

Gift subscription address _____

_____ Postcode _____

Please send to the above, beginning with the May 2000 issue:

(please tick box)	UK	SURFACE	AIR MAIL
NEW DAYLIGHT	❑ £10.20	❑ £11.55	❑ £13.50
NEW DAYLIGHT 3-year sub	❑ £25.00		

Please complete the payment details below and send your coupon, with appropriate payment to: **The Bible Reading Fellowship, Peter's Way, Sandy Lane West, Oxford OX4 5HG**

Your name _____

Your address _____

_____ Postcode _____

Total enclosed £ _____ (cheques should be made payable to 'BRF')

Payment by cheque ❑ postal order ❑ Visa ❑ Mastercard ❑ Switch ❑

Card number: ☐☐☐☐ ☐☐☐☐ ☐☐☐☐ ☐☐☐☐

Expiry date of card: ☐☐☐☐ Issue number (Switch): ☐☐☐☐

Signature (essential if paying by credit/Switch card) _____

NB: BRF notes are also available from your local Christian bookshop. **BRF is a Registered Charity**

Books by Margaret Cundiff

Living by the Book
A personal journey through the Sermon on the Mount

'If everybody lived by the Sermon on the Mount,' said the man on the train, 'the world would be a better place.'

This remark started Margaret Cundiff on a journey of exploration to rediscover those chapters of Matthew's Gospel that we think we know so well. It was, she found, a sometimes risky process, challenging our most basic assumptions about how we live our lives, and demanding honest answers to hard questions.

Join Margaret in discovering what Jesus really says about the good life, and what it involves for those who set out to follow him. Is it possible for ordinary Christians to live by the Book? What happens if we don't? What happens if we do?

The Cost of Living
A personal journey in John's Gospel

The Cost of Living is a personal journey of discovery in the final chapters of John's Gospel, from the point when Jesus raises his friend Lazarus from the dead and then starts on the road to Calvary. In a series of accessible reflections, Margaret Cundiff delves into these chapters to help us discover what it means—and what it costs—when we choose to follow Jesus on this road.

The book of John is in many ways the most demanding, yet one of the best-loved, of the Gospels. Many Christians may be so familiar with the words that the great theological arguments behind them can be over looked, while those reading for the first time may equally miss out on the deep truths. The Cost of Living provides an opportunity for both kinds of readers to encounter the Bible story afresh.

See overleaf for an order form for both books.